LAN Traffic Management

Hewlett-Packard Professional Books

GRADY Practical software metrics for project management and process improvement

GROSVENOR, ICHIRO, O'BRIEN Mainframe downsizing to upside your business: IT-preneuring

HELSEL Cutting your test development time with HP VEE: An iconic programming language

MADEIL, PARSONS, ABEGG Developing and localizing international software

PONIATOWSKI The HP-UX system administrator's 'how to' book

WITTE Electronic test instruments

WITTE Spectral network measurements

LAN Traffic Management

Peter Phaal

Prentice Hall
New York London Toronto Sydney Tokyo Singapore

First published 1994 by
Prentice Hall International (UK) Ltd
Campus 400, Maylands Avenue
Hemel Hempstead
Hertfordshire, HP2 7EZ
A division of
Simon & Schuster International Group

Typeset in 10 pt Times
by Columns Design and Production Services Ltd, Reading, UK

Printed and bound in Great Britain at the University Press, Cambridge

Library of Congress Cataloging-in-Publication Data

Phaal, Peter.
LAN traffic management / Peter Phaal.
p. cm. – (Hewlett-Packard professional books)
ISBN 0–13–124207–5 (pbk.)
1. Local area networks (Computer networks)
2. Telecommunication – Traffic – Management.
I. Title. II. Series.
TK5105.7.P49 1994 94–7848
004.6'8–dc20 CIP

British Library Cataloguing in Publication Data

A catalogue record for this book is available from the British Library
ISBN 0–13124207–5 (pbk)

2 3 4 5 98 97 96 95 94

To Karen

Contents

1 Introduction

Why does my network operate so slowly? Do I need a faster network? Is my network congested? What can I do to reduce congestion? If you have ever asked these questions or tried to build software tools to help answer them then this book is for you.

Traffic management is becoming an important issue as workstation and personal computer networking speeds start to outstrip the capacity of current and emerging network technologies. Only a few years ago most local area networks (LANs) were lightly loaded. As they now approach saturation it is important to tune the network to traffic patterns in order to avoid congestive collapse.

This book discusses the tasks facing LAN administrators as they try to manage the flow of traffic on their network and adapt the network to cope with changing demands. It covers subjects as diverse as network design, the use of routers, bridges and hubs, monitoring, troubleshooting and even accounting. There are many books about network management, but it seems that the practical problems of traffic management facing the site administrator have been largely overlooked.

It is worth saying a little about what this book is not. Although many of the ideas discussed have general application, this book is not a general introduction to networking or network management; it is assumed that the reader will be familiar with the basic concepts in these areas. This book does not concern itself with wide area network (WAN) design or management – there are many good reference books on these subjects.

The main theme of this book is the management of traffic flows within the local area. This restricts the discussion to networks in a limited geographical area such as a building or campus. The aim is to understand the way in which traffic flows on such LANs and the way in which it can be controlled and managed with the appropriate network infrastructure and tools. This is an area that is often neglected; few network managers properly understand what demands their users place on their network or the types of simple changes that should be made. Good traffic management can lower costs while at the same time improving performance, reliability and security. As LANs become an integral part of many businesses these factors become increasingly important. By the end of this book you should be able to implement a traffic management strategy that will show immediate and significant benefits.

There are four main sections to the book. To start with we examine the objectives of traffic management and strategies for achieving them. In so doing we identify activities that take place on different time scales. The remaining three sections deal with these activities. The first deals with longer term strategic activities, including issues such as network design and planning for growth. Short term or operational management follows in the next section and includes activities such as congestion management and troubleshooting. Finally, it is impossible to manage a network if you don't monitor what is going on so the fourth and final section is concerned with network monitoring.

Many practical examples are given to illustrate the points made in this book. The Hewlett-Packard Embedded Advanced Sampling Environment (HP EASE) traffic management system is used to provide these examples. However, the discussion and examples are very general and it is not necessary to be familiar with these products.

2 Network management framework

'Why spend time on network management?' If you are asking this question, rather than 'How can I spend less time on network management?' then it is likely that you only have a small network.

2.1 The complexity 'wall'

The problem with networks, and many other types of system, is that as they get larger they also get more complicated. What makes it even worse is that the complexity doesn't simply grow in proportion to the network size, the complexity tends to grow exponentially (see Figure 2.1). For example doubling a network's size could make it not twice, but many more times more complicated to manage.

The reason for this exponential growth is that the various components in the network interact. As a very simple example, imagine a network consisting of two connected machines A and B (see Figure 2.2). The two possible interactions are A talks to B and B talks to A.

If we add two more machines C and D (see Figure 2.3) there are additional interactions C talks to D, D talks to C, which doubles it, but the additional interactions A talks to C, A talks to D, B talks to C, B talks to D, C talks to A, C talks to B, D talks to A and finally D talks to B, giving a total of 12. In this case doubling the network size increased the number of possible interactions and the complexity by 6 times.

This problem of rapidly increasing complexity as the system gets bigger demonstrates itself in many ways. Throughout this chapter we will be using analogies from business management to illustrate network management issues.

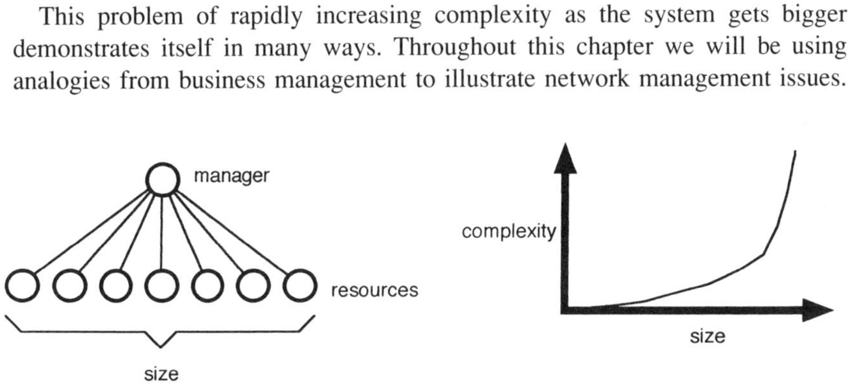

Figure 2.1
Management complexity increases with system size.

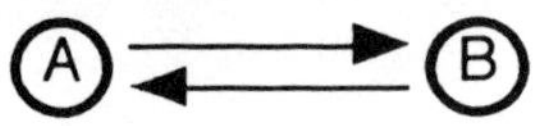

Figure 2.2
Interactions between two machines.

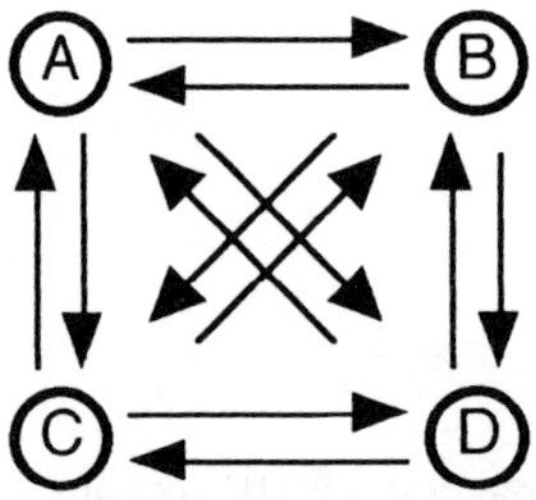

Figure 2.3
Interactions between four machines.

These principles are very general and apply to many types of system. In this case an interesting analogy is with the formation and growth of companies. Many growing companies fail when they reach a certain size because of the failure of management systems to keep up with the rapidly increasing complexity of the business. To keep growing the company needs to put in place management structures that allow it to cope with the increased complexity. In networking the problem is similar. A small network is relatively simple and doesn't require much in the way of network management. As the network grows a point is reached at which a small increase in size suddenly increases the complexity beyond the capabilities of the existing management structure, or lack of it, and the cost of downtime and troubleshooting becomes unacceptable. The network can be grown cost effectively beyond this point if appropriate network management strategies are put in place (see Figure 2.4).

The task of network management is to reduce the complexity of running large diverse networks. We can assess the power of a management solution by the degree to which it simplifies the management task. The techniques described throughout the rest of this book all try to reduce complexity in different ways. This is the major challenge in managing large networks.

2.2 Define objectives

The first thing to do before developing a network management strategy is to decide what management objectives need to be achieved.

Traffic management is unlike most other aspects of network management in that it most directly deals with the use of the network and understanding the requirements of the users. Other areas of network management such as fault, inventory, security or configuration management are important, but they tend to be more concerned with the technical and administrative tasks of dealing with networking equipment.

Ideas from quality management can help to define traffic management objectives. One of the key concepts of quality management is that the results are measured by customers. For a network manager the customers are the users of the

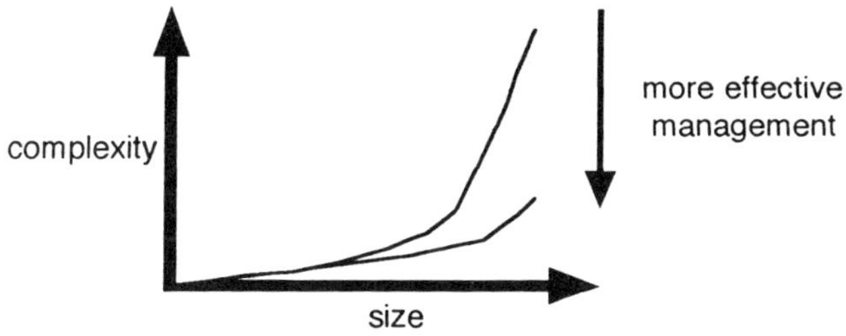

Figure 2.4
Effective management strategies reduce complexity.

network. Understanding the users of the network, their behaviour, their needs and how they are being met is a vital first step in providing a high quality network service.

It is easy to view users with suspicion and focus on the technical tasks of network management. This results in networks that may be technically elegant, but which fail to meet user requirements. In the long term the network (and its management) will be judged not on technical merits, but on the degree to which it serves users.

Obviously there are important budgetary and personnel constraints. The challenge is to provide a high quality service while meeting these constraints. In dealing with costs it is important to realise that most of the cost of a local area network is made up of the cost of the people needed to run it and not the cost of the network components. Often the true personnel costs are hidden because users or volunteers unofficially perform many of the management tasks. This is usually a very expensive and poor way to provide network management. It is worth giving someone official responsibility for the network and making the investment in planning and network infrastructure so that the network is cost effective to operate rather than concentrating the cost of the components.

Other important ideas from quality management are those of continual improvement and education. Many of the objectives of quality management can only be achieved by continuous monitoring. As the network manager learns more about the network and its users, changes can be made to gradually improve the quality of the network service. Part of the task of the manager is to train users so that they understand enough about the network to act responsibly and can make best use of it.

Once the basic objectives have been determined and adequate resources allocated, a number of techniques can be applied to simplify the management tasks.

2.3 Hierarchical decomposition

An important strategy for reducing management complexity is hierarchical decomposition. Hierarchical decomposition involves combining network resources together into small groups. These groups are in turn combined. This continues until only one group is left. This 'tree' of groups is then the hierarchical decomposition of the network management system (see Figure 2.5).

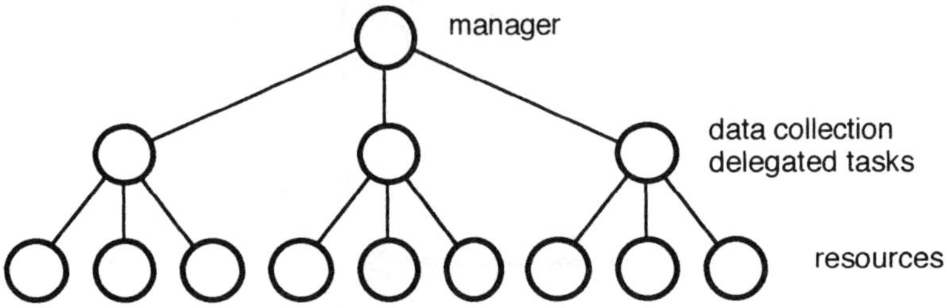

Figure 2.5
Hierarchical management.

Typically the machines within each department are grouped to form workgroups, these workgroups are then grouped to form sites and the sites are grouped to form the corporate network.

The reason why hierarchical decomposition works is that the large system is broken up into a number of smaller subsystems, each of which has manageable complexity (remember that complexity increases exponentially with system size). In Figure 2.5 instead of trying to manage nine nodes directly the network is divided into three parts, each management subsystem consisting of three nodes and thus much simpler to manage. As far as the top-level manager is concerned the management task is now simplified to that of managing three subsystems, rather than the nine end nodes.

This strategy is familiar to anyone in business. Human resources are organised hierarchically with workers reporting to project managers, who report to department managers, who report to section managers and so on. This greatly simplifies the task of any single manager and makes possible the formation of large organisations.

2.4 Functional decomposition

Another way of simplifying management is to split up activities along functional boundaries. The idea is that there are activities or functions that can be separated because they interact only weakly. The key to good functional decomposition is making sure that interactions are weak. Examples of how this strategy is used in business are the division of activities and people into areas such as sales, marketing, accounting, research and development and manufacturing.

In network management activities can be divided into loosely coupled areas such as troubleshooting, access control, traffic management and configuration management. There is interaction between these areas, but it is weak and it is possible to manage them largely independently. Functional decomposition works for much the same reason as hierarchical decomposition. The task is divided into smaller more manageable pieces.

2.5 Frequency decomposition

Another way of splitting up tasks is to look at the frequency with which they take place. The tasks that take place frequently are often very different from and can be separated from tasks that occur less frequently. This more action-oriented view of network management can be captured by looking at network management as a feedback process aimed at controlling the network. Different feedback loops operate at different intervals and control different aspects of the network behaviour.

The control model in Figure 2.6 starts with monitoring as an activity. If you don't monitor then you won't see any problems develop and be able to take any effective action. The purpose of the monitoring activity is to provide a central view of the current network state and over time the network history.

The state and history are key points of integration for the various short term and long term activities. Short term activities are those that take place in time scales of minutes and hours. They are aimed at detecting problems, identifying their cause and fixing them. The short term activities involve comparing the network state with policies determining what is acceptable service and taking appropriate actions on the network to resolve problems. The policies may also specify what these actions should be and describe escalation procedures if problems are serious. These activities could also include scheduled maintenance determined at the long term level.

The long term activities take place over days, weeks and longer periods. Long term management involves such activities as the design of the network, changes to configuration to partition traffic, buying policy and adding redundancy to improve reliability. These tasks are performed over periods of weeks and months and the results of making long term changes take time to assess.

A major difference between short term and long term management is that short term management tends to be reactive and long term management proactive. In a well managed network most problems should be anticipated and corrected before they become serious. The short term, reactive, management is only there to deal with unpredictable problems.

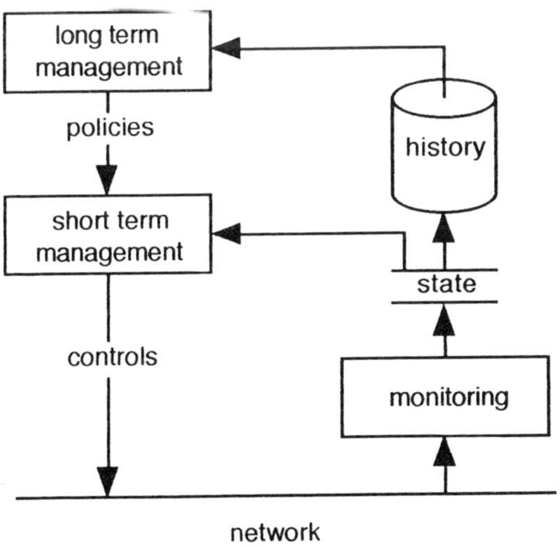

Figure 2.6
Control model of management.

Again these techniques are widely employed in other areas such as business management. There are tactical decisions made on a day to day basis responding to recently collected information to correct short term problems, such as a customer complaint, or a lost shipment. Longer term strategic activities include the tracking of demand, the planning of new advertising campaigns and the construction of new manufacturing capacity. Feedback is used to monitor the effect of decisions and allow adjustments to be made so that desired results are obtained.

This continuous monitoring and control model also fits in well with the idea of continuous improvement mentioned as part of quality management.

2.6 Management architecture

The previous ideas might sound fine in theory, but how can they be put into practice? Before going on to describe the architecture it is important to remember that while good tools are an important part of the story it is people who put them to use and make the process of management work. Keep in mind the organisational procedures that need to be put in place to implement these processes and to make best use of the tools.

Let's look at some of the key elements of a traffic management architecture. The Hewlett-Packard Embedded Advanced Sampling Environment (HP EASE) family of tools illustrate the application of the various decomposition techniques (hierarchical, functional and frequency) and demonstrate a simple architecture for building scalable network management systems.

Figure 2.7 shows some of the key elements of a traffic management system. The diagram divides vertically and horizontally. The vertical divisions correspond to a hierarchical decomposition, separating the many devices in the network from the distributed monitoring services that monitor them and the applications that make use of the collected data. The horizontal divisions identify some of the functional areas of management such as status monitoring, topology discovery and traffic monitoring. Manageable network devices such as hubs, bridges and routers have software running on them, called an agent, that responds to management commands and allows them to be controlled and monitored. Each service makes use of agent functions to construct part of the network state and history. The applications use this information to provide operational and strategic control of the network.

In addition to the scalability benefits of this division of network management into a number of services and applications, there are some other advantages over a more closely integrated approach. New services can be added over time and services from different vendors can be combined to produce the overall system. This means that the traffic management services provided by HP EASE can easily be combined with existing management systems that perform other management tasks such as fault management.

The applications shown in the diagram are those most directly associated with traffic management. The lines show data flows and the applications can be

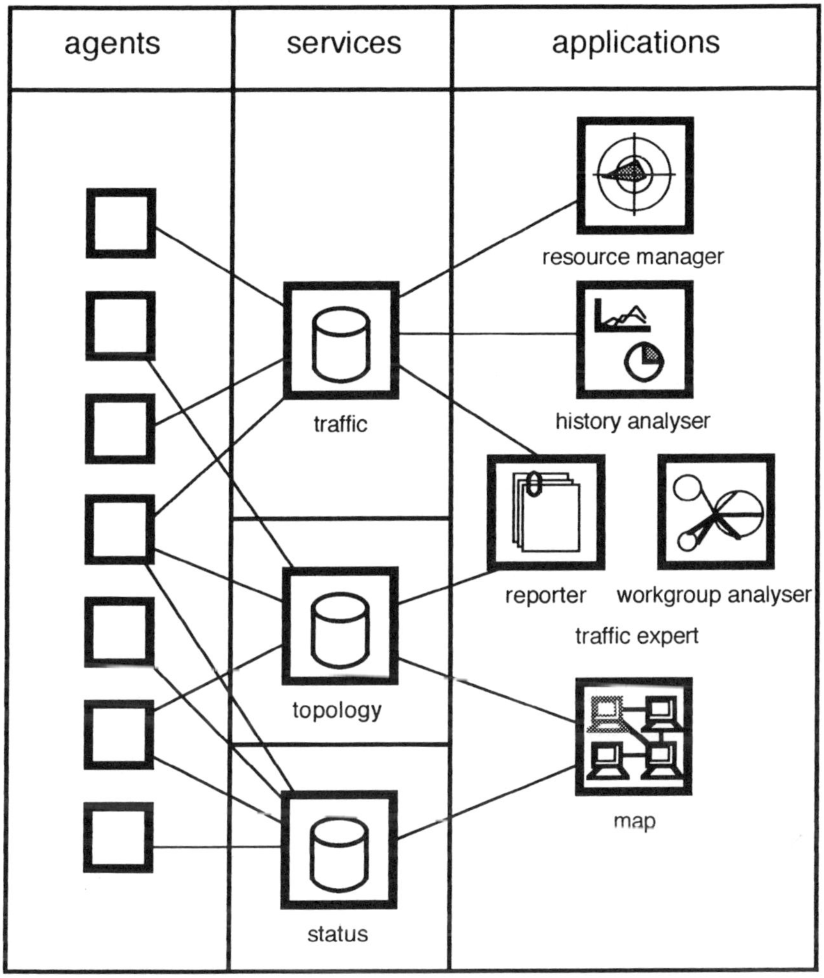

Figure 2.7
Agents, services and applications.

grouped together according to their dependence on different monitoring services. The map application could be any of a number of currently available network management applications that display a map of the network, allow various network devices to be remotely controlled and display status information by the use of colour (red indicating a fault and green for healthy). The HP OpenView Interconnect Manager[1] provides this type of functionality. The remaining applications access traffic information. Both the HP Resource Manager[2] and HP History Analyzer[3] require only traffic information in order to operate. The two

[1] HP 27361A OpenView Interconnect Manager 700/800.
[2] HP J2345A OpenView Resource Manager/UNIX.
[3] HP J2347A OpenView History Analyzer/UNIX.

applications making up the HP Traffic Expert[4] relate traffic and topology together and make use of information from both of these collection services.

2.7 Applications and tasks

A different perspective on the traffic management applications is to consider the way in which they are used together to perform complicated tasks. Each application is designed for a single type of job, rather than to be general purpose. These applications can then be used together to complete complicated tasks. This approach differs from that of building highly integrated, general purpose, network management systems. The difference is analogous to the difference between a box of tools and a Swiss army knife – the Swiss army knife has everything, but you really wouldn't want to build a house with it.

In Figure 2.8 the major grouping is to separate short term and long term activities. The arrows show the way in which the use of the applications is linked when performing common traffic management tasks.

The map application should give a clear indication of the current status of the devices in the network, with any failed devices clearly shown in red. It should also provide the information and control functions needed to take action when a problem is spotted. What is missing is a clear idea of the current level of congestion in the network. While the map might show that everything is up (green) this doesn't necessarily mean that there aren't severe congestion problems.

Detecting and locating congestion problems is the major task of the Resource Manager. It constantly monitors all the many segments in the network and presents a single display that shows, network wide, whether there is any congestion.

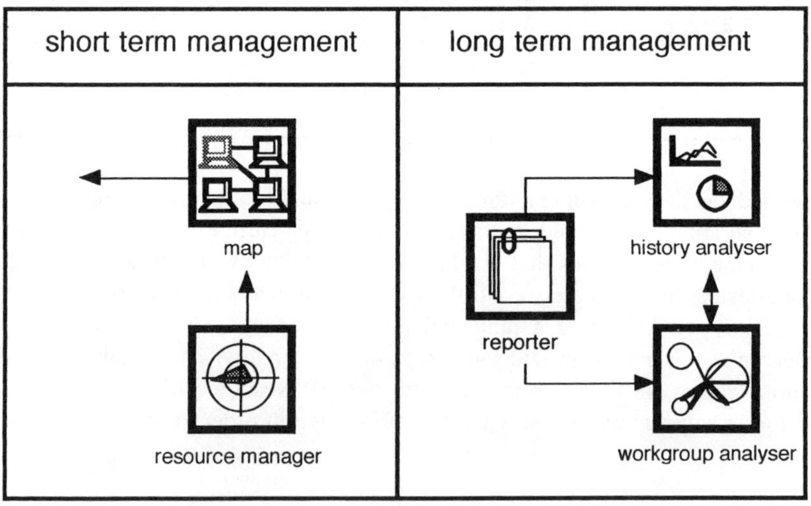

Figure 2.8
Long and short term tasks and applications.

[4] HP J2348A OpenView Traffic Expert/UNIX.

It also supports the ability quickly to find out where in the network the problem is located and rapidly identifies the sources of the problem so that action can be taken (possibly using information or controls available in the map). Together the two applications take care of the tasks of short term traffic management.

Long term activities take place on a daily, weekly and monthly basis. Continuous traffic monitoring produces large amounts of data and finding useful information within this data can be difficult. The Reporter periodically looks through all the data. It identifies unusual traffic, significant changes and even suggests improvements to the network that will reduce congestion before it becomes a problem. The areas that the Reporter identifies as needing further attention can then be examined in detail using the two analysis tools.

The History Analyzer allows traffic to be examined as it changes over time so that the evolution of problems can be seen and their long term significance assessed. The Workgroup Analyzer allows the relationship between the network topology and traffic to be examined and is particularly useful for judging the impact of possible changes of topology. In many cases both forms of analysis are needed in order fully to understand a problem.

Together these applications provide a reasonably complete traffic management toolkit. Each application is specialised to perform a particular task, but when used together most problems can be solved.

2.8 Application techniques

There are a number of ideas that can be incorporated in management applications and procedures in order to make them more effective. Most of the techniques involve reducing complexity by helping to identify and present significant information.

2.8.1 *Tell a story*

Think of any management action as a story. It has a beginning, a middle and an end. The beginning usually involves the identification of an issue, the middle the exploration of that issue in order to understand causes, possible actions and their consequences, and finally the end involves the selection and execution of one of these actions. A good management support tool should fit easily into this type of story. How does it help detect problems, explore options and implement choices? Many poorly designed applications provide all the mechanisms needed to perform a task, but do not link them together to make the task simple to perform. A task focused application will streamline the decision process, making the information required at each stage easily available, making it hard to make mistakes.

This idea is also a very useful way to design applications. Think of a few key scenarios or stories that capture the essence of the activities that the application is to support. These scenarios can be used to create a story board that links together the different displays that the proposed tools will present. For each display find out what question it answers and what questions it is likely to cause the user to ask. If a display doesn't answer questions from the scenario – remove it. If there are questions from the scenario that are not answered by any display – try to modify an existing display or add a new one that answers the question. Make it easy to go from displays that ask questions to those that answer them. Continue this process until all questions within the scope of the scenario have been asked and answered. This results in a task focused style of interface that is easy to explain and use.

Another way of thinking about scenarios is that they explore cause and effect, answering such questions as 'What am I seeing?', 'How did I measure it?', 'Is it a problem?' and 'What are its causes?'

2.8.2 *Find the odd one out*

A powerful technique for monitoring is that of finding extremes of behaviour. In any large system with many similar components, such as a network, it is possible to find problems by looking for individual components that differ significantly from their peers. Because problems tend to be rare and cause unusual behaviour they show up as outliers when similar devices are compared. One of the nice features of this technique is that tools using it automatically adapt to the normal behaviour of the system that they are monitoring. Another important property is the ability to detect classes of problem that were not envisioned by the designer of the application – a big limitation of many current systems.

2.8.3 *Fix major problems first*

This technique is known by many names: Pareto analysis, the principle of diminishing returns or the 80/20 rule. The basic idea is that the main contributors to a problem or issue should be tackled before looking at the smaller contributors. Typically the biggest one or two contributors are responsible for most of the problem. This produces the largest benefit for the minimum effort.

The technique combines well with the use of scenarios. By constructing displays that show the main contributors to key management measures, applications can be designed that are highly effective. Displaying only the top contributors significantly reduces the amount of information that must be presented. As long as the metric is meaningful the top five contributors, say, are usually sufficient and much easier to interpret than the entire list.

2.8.4 *Watch for changes*

Problems are often caused by changes to the network. By keeping a constant track of changes it is often possible to identify the cause of a problem by looking at the changes that immediately preceded it. Conversely, looking for sudden changes in network behaviour will help to detect changes to the network that could cause problems. This technique can be used to reduce significantly the amount of information presented by applications.

2.8.5 *Tight control means small changes*

One of the major benefits of looking at network management as a continuous feedback process, as we did when we developed the control model, is that it can be used to simplify applications.

To understand why this is so, imagine that we have been running a management system like that described in the control model. The control loops act to bring the network close to an ideal and so if they have been doing their job the network should be close to this target. All that the management system then needs to do is detect small changes from the ideal and correct these small problems, bringing the network back under control. Detecting and managing small changes from a known target is a much simpler task than trying to deal with all possible problems in all possible configurations. This sounds fine, but there is a catch – in order for it to work the network must first be brought under control. However, this only needs to be done once when the control system is put in place; after that the control system will ensure that it stays close to its target.

This is a phenomenon that should be familiar to managers. It is much simpler to make frequent, small corrections to a project than to wait until there are large problems and to try and fix things then.

2.8.6 *Take a network level view*

Networks are much more than a collection of connected devices. Many of their functions can only be understood by looking at the way in which these devices work together to move data. The idea of the network level view is to think of ways of looking at network information that allow these relationships to be better understood and managed. It may be necessary to look at the network in a number of different ways in order fully to understand all the issues involved in making a change. By only showing devices that relate to a particular function, and only those aspects of the devices needed to perform that function, it is possible to construct simple interfaces to what would otherwise be very difficult tasks.

2.8.7 *Measure, don't guess*

Many network management applications are complicated, simulating the complexity of the network. Simulations are only as good as the data that they are given, they do not scale well and produce results that need careful interpretation. Direct measurement removes the guesswork and allows much simpler tools to make far more accurate predictions than would otherwise be possible.

A number of different ideas have been presented in this chapter, many of which may seem quite abstract. The following chapters should help to demonstrate the practical application of these techniques as long and short term traffic management and traffic monitoring are discussed.

3 Long term management

Strategic traffic management is concerned with ensuring that there is sufficient capacity in the network to provide an acceptable level of service to users while minimising costs. This objective highlights a number of important management tasks. We need to state clearly what level of service we want to provide and then we need some way to determine whether we are successfully delivering that service. Understanding user demand helps to determine the service level.

An important property of strategic management is that it is proactive. Problems need to be anticipated and corrective action taken before they become serious. This is particularly important when planning network growth because there can be a significant lead time involved in making changes. If changes are only made in response to problems then there can be extended periods of unacceptable performance.

This process of setting quality objectives and continually monitoring and improving the service is known as quality control. Figure 3.1 shows the steps of monitoring, planning, assessing options and making changes as a continuous cycle. In the long term it can significantly improve the quality of the services delivered and reduce the cost of delivery.

3.1 Design for manageability

Measurement is a key component of management and suitable measurement and reporting systems must be designed into the network to provide the continuous monitoring needed for proactive management. The benefits of having manageable components easily justifies their higher cost when used in large networks. It

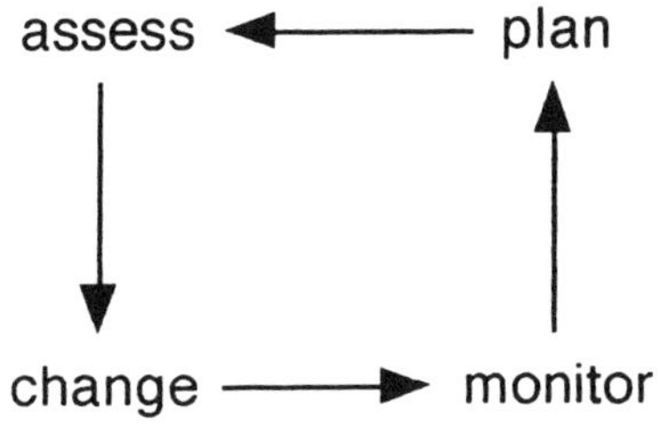

Figure 3.1
Strategic management process.

is worth thinking ahead, many smaller networks end up growing rapidly, and it can be expensive to try and add network management later. Management functionality in network devices will only be useful if good network management applications are also available and are incorporated in the day to day management routine.

Selecting good quality components and controlling the installation and configuration of equipment is an important way of preventing problems. A large number of network problems are caused by unreliable components, poor installation and devices that do not meet the required specifications. These problems can be very difficult to track down and it best to avoid them. This is an area where spending a little extra money initially will save a lot more later on.

Many of the solutions to traffic problems involve making changes to the network configuration. Designing the network so that it is easy to change is vital, otherwise you will be powerless to make the changes needed to avoid emerging problems. Part of the administrative responsibility is keeping an accurate record of the network configuration and the changes that are made.

3.2 Protocol layering

Before discussing the different types of connectivity device it is worth quickly reviewing some of the basic concepts of protocol layering. Getting data reliably across a network requires a number of different functions to be performed by the communicating machines. The functions have been organised hierarchically in layers so that different implementations of each function can be combined. A particular implementation of a functional layer is referred to as a protocol. Exchanging data is made possible by combining protocol layers to form a protocol stack.

The operation of connectivity devices can be explained in terms of the first three layers in the stack. A brief description of the functions of these layers follows.

3.2.1 Physical layer (e.g. fibre, twisted pair, coaxial cable)

The first problem in connecting machines together is to make sure that they have compatible connectors, compatible wiring and that they agree on the signals to send. The physical layer definition deals with these issues.

3.2.2 Media access layer (e.g. Ethernet,[5] Token Ring, FDDI)

If machines are physically connected together the next problem is to decide when each machine can send data, who is meant to receive it, who sent it, at what speed to send it and whether or not the information has been corrupted.

[5] Ethernet is a trademark of Xerox Corp.

In order to achieve these objectives the data is formed into blocks called frames (see Figure 3.2). The frames have source (X) and destination (Y) addresses to identify the interfaces involved in the data exchange. A CRC (cyclic redundancy code) is added to the end of the frame so that the station receiving it can tell if the data has been corrupted. Most common LAN media access protocols make use of six byte MAC (Media ACcess) addresses. There are special types of destination address called broadcast and multicast addresses. In the case of the broadcast address, all interfaces will receive the frame. Multicast addresses are similar to the broadcast address in that they are delivered to each interface, but in this case an interface can decide whether it wants to receive a particular multicast address.

Frames usually have upper and lower limits on the amount of data they may contain. The upper limit bounds the time that a single machine can occupy the network before allowing others to send. The lower limit on frame size is determined by the size of the address and CRC fields and any other MAC information, as well as by timing constraints in the MAC protocol.

3.2.3 *Network layer (e.g. IP, IPX, AppleTalk[6])*

Providing end to end exchange of information may involve crossing many links. These links may have different frame sizes and formats. The network layer protocols provide mechanisms for navigating a path or route between the two end machines. This routing function is supported by having special network-level addresses for each machine. These addresses usually have two parts, an area, subnetwork or zone identifier that specifies a general region in the overall network, and a station part that specifies the machine within that area.

The network source (x) and destination (y) addresses are combined with data in order to form a packet (see Figure 3.3). Packets may be larger than the frame size supported by the underlying media access level and so mechanisms are needed to break up the packet into pieces before sending them and for putting the pieces back together at the receiver. This process is termed fragmentation and reassembly.

Layers have been defined above the network layer (the transport, session, presentation and application layers), but these are not relevant to the following discussion of LAN connectivity devices.

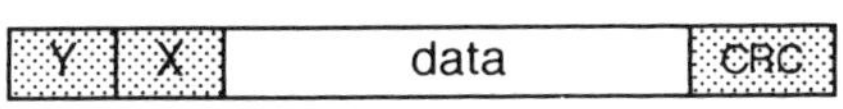

Figure 3.2
Features of a media access layer frame.

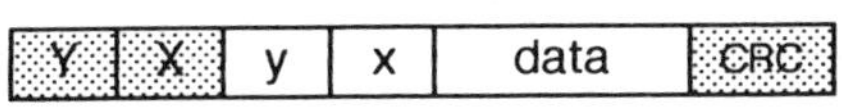

Figure 3.3
Network layer packet contained in media access layer frame.

[6] AppleTalk is a trademark of Apple Computer, Inc.

3.3 Connectivity devices

Connectivity devices are used to connect different pieces of the network together. Without them it would be impossible to construct large networks. As well as providing connectivity these devices are also important points of management control. We will be discussing the different types of connectivity device and the way in which they can be used to control traffic.

3.3.1 Directly connected

Before discussing connectivity devices let's look at the simple case of two nodes directly connected together (see Figure 3.4). This will work if each node has compatible physical, media access and network layers.

3.3.2 Repeaters, hubs and concentrators

Many physical media types such as twisted pair or fibre-optic cable only connect pairs of interfaces; others like coaxial cable have limits on the number of interfaces that can be connected, but allow a number of interfaces to be connected. Physical connections also have limits on the distance that they can cover. In order to overcome these limitations a simple device can be constructed that has a number of physical interfaces, each of which can have a different physical connection (see Figure 3.5). This type of connectivity device may be called a hub, a repeater or a concentrator. It works by simply repeating everything it receives on each interface to all other interfaces.

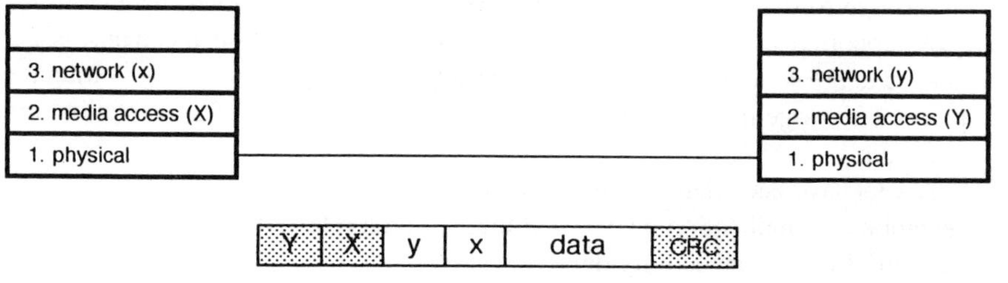

Figure 3.4
Directly connected machines transferring a packet (packet received while being sent).

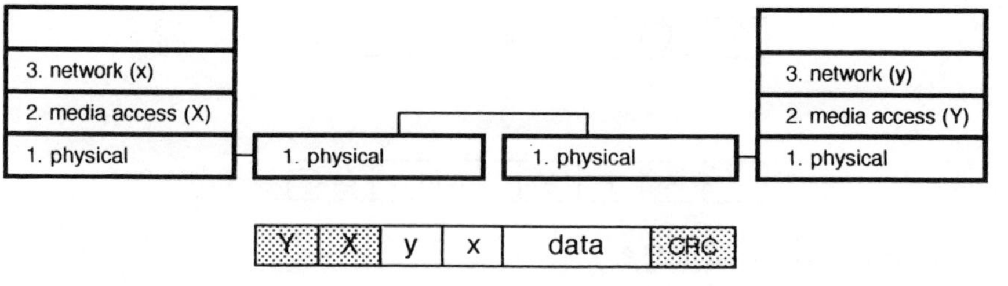

Figure 3.5
Machines connected to a repeater transferring a packet (repeater resends packet while receiving it).

Repeaters do not need to interpret any part of the fames that they receive and so start resending a frame while still receiving it. This means that there is a very low delay for a frame crossing a repeater (usually only the time taken to receive a few bits). It also keeps the cost of repeaters low since they do not need to provide any storage.

Repeaters can be connected together to form larger networks. They can also make it possible to mix physical connection types, for example to connect machines on coaxial cable to others on twisted pair wiring.

Because all traffic is sent to all interfaces by a repeater, the bandwidth of a network connected by repeaters is shared. The media access protocols ensure that the bandwidth is shared fairly. This also means that all interfaces connected together by repeaters must use the same media access protocol.

Although repeaters can be connected together to form large networks, there is usually a limit on how many are allowed to be connected and thus how big the network can be. This limit is usually to do with timing constraints in the media access protocol. Also because all the machines connected together by repeaters share the same bandwidth the network can become congested as the number of machines increases.

Repeaters are limited in their ability to isolate errors. Because a repeater doesn't examine the frames, but simply copies them it will copy frames that have been corrupted, wasting bandwidth and allowing one bad physical interface to cause problems throughout the network.

3.3.3 *Bridges*

Adding a media access layer to the connectivity device so that it receives the frame and can look at the source, destination and error checking information before resending it creates a device called a bridge (see Figure 3.6).

Because the bridge looks at the destination address of the frame it can be smart about resending it. There is no point resending a frame if both the source and destination interfaces are connected to the same bridge interface. If the bridge has many interfaces it can choose to resend the frame only on the interface connected to the destination. Bridges can be smart and discover where interfaces are based on the source addresses in the frames; this type of bridge is called a 'learning' bridge. The bridge must forward all the broadcast and multicast frames so that interfaces that want to receive them can.

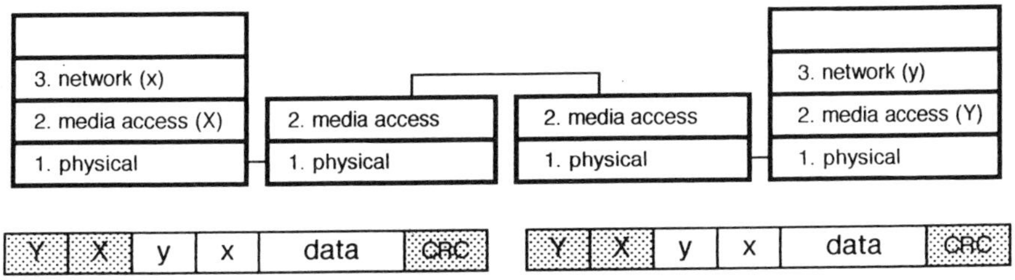

Figure 3.6
Machines connected by a bridge transferring a frame (bridge receives entire frame before resending it unchanged).

Bridges provide better error isolation than repeaters because they look at the error detection code in the frame and don't forward corrupt frames.

Bridges are limited when trying to connect media access layers of different types. The addressing schemes used in the different frame types may be incompatible and because fragmentation and reassembly is performed at the network layer there can be difficulties if maximum frame sizes are different between the media access protocols.

3.3.4 Routers

Adding a network layer to the connectivity device makes its function independent of the different media access protocols (see Figure 3.7). This type of device is called a router.

Routers receive and send frames on different media access interfaces and so the source machine must know to send packets to the router's MAC address. The router in turn will use its own MAC address when sending the packet on to the destination machine. Most network protocols use a broadcast mechanism, called address resolution, in order to determine the MAC address to send packets to for a given destination network address.

Routers are concerned with the end to end delivery of packets. When they receive a frame they strip off the media access information, examine the packet addressing information and, based on routing information, decide which interface to resend the packet on. The packet may then move from router to router until it reaches its destination. As long as the source and destination machines run the same network protocol they can easily communicate even if they use different media access protocols.

Routers will not forward MAC broadcast and multicast frames. This can be useful in big networks where the number of broadcasts and multicasts can get quite large.

Routers are the highest level connectivity device, the higher protocol layers run on the computers attached to the network. This makes the router an important point of control because it has a high level view of the traffic and usually occupies strategic positions in the network. Routers are also attractive as points of control because they are administered by the network manager whereas the networked computers are often administered by different people. Routers usually provide a number of advanced management features such as traffic account-

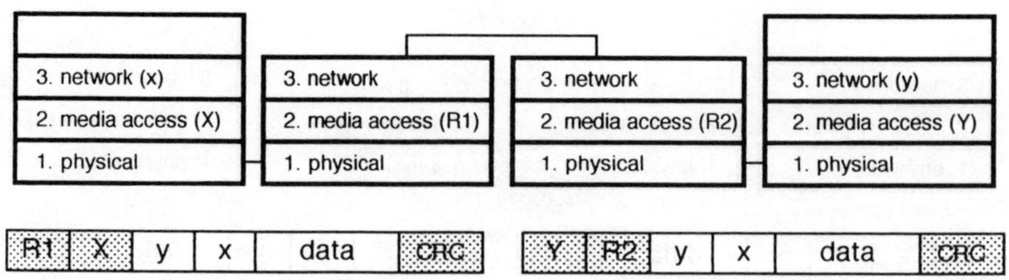

Figure 3.7
Machines connected by a router transferring a packet (router receives entire packet before resending it with changed MAC).

ing and packet filtering. Unfortunately, performance usually suffers when using these advanced features.

Most routers can also act as a bridge. This is important because not all protocols can be routed, but again this usually significantly reduces performance.

3.4 Common physical media

This section mentions the most popular physical media used in local area networks and comments briefly on their manageability. The choice of physical media and the rules governing installation are well beyond the scope of this book. The correct installation standards should be followed when installing cabling. Bad cabling can cause a wide variety of problems that are difficult to detect and correct.

3.4.1 *Twisted pair*

Twisted pair wiring comes in two main flavours, shielded and unshielded. Unshielded twisted pair wiring is the same type that is used for telephone wiring in many countries. Because it is the same as phone wiring it can be conveniently switched between different uses. It is possible to operate a phone, terminal or local area network over the same wires. It is its flexibility and low cost that has made this type of physical connection so popular. Shielded twisted pair is more expensive but can, in theory, be used to carry higher data rates.

Twisted pair wiring provides a point to point link. Hubs are needed to connect the wires together to form a network. The hub provides isolation if a problem occurs with one of the links, preventing it from affecting other links. The use of twisted pair structured wiring is described later in this chapter.

3.4.2 *Coaxial cable*

There is a large installed base of coaxial cable, although it is less popular than twisted pair for new installations. There are two main types of coaxial cable in common use. Thick cable is expensive and difficult to connect to but allows greater distances to be covered. It is typically used as the backbone connecting different parts of the site together. Thin cable is cheap and easy to use and is typically used within a localised area. New machines can easily be added by extending the cable.

The main problem with coaxial cable from a management standpoint is that if there is a fault anywhere along its length all the machines attached to it will be affected. Thin coaxial cable is still a cheap and simple way to build a small network.

3.4.3 *Optical fibre*

Fibre-optic cable operates as a point to point link. Fibre links can be used to cover large distances and are immune to electrical noise and earthing problems.

This makes fibre particularly useful when going between buildings since it provides protection against lightning and is capable of covering the distance between the buildings.

3.5 Common media access protocols

This section makes some basic observations on the performance of common media access protocols. There have been extensive debates about the relative merits of different protocols, but basically they all perform reasonably well. There are differences in basic speed, difficulty of configuration, popularity, cost and cabling that can determine choices, but from a traffic management standpoint they are similar.

3.5.1 Ethernet and 802.3

Ethernet is a simple, popular protocol that is widely available from a number of vendors. It provides a 10 Mbit/s data rate and contrary to popular belief performs well under high load. There were some initial theoretical studies that predicted that Ethernets would not work well if loaded above 30%. This has been shown not to be the case and there are currently many Ethernets working well at much higher loads (90% is not unusual). There are currently a number of proposals for standards that will provide 100 Mbit/s Ethernet.

A machine that wants to send data on an Ethernet waits until the network is quiet and then starts sending. If two or more machines start sending at the same time then a collision occurs and all the machines involved stop sending and try again a random period of time later. This process is repeated until the data gets through. The collision mechanism is a normal part of the protocol and quickly resolves the contention so that each machine gets a fair share of the network. The timing requirements of collision detection limit the geographical size of a single Ethernet. Bridges and routers can be used to connect Ethernets together to increase the network size.

There are two main flavours of this protocol that can coexist on the same network, Ethernet and 802.3. Ethernet was developed by Digital, Intel and Xerox and this original version is still the most popular. 802.3 is a standard based on Ethernet that was developed by the Institute for Electrical and Electronics Engineers (IEEE).

The Ethernet protocol can be used with coaxial, twisted pair and fibre optic cables.

3.5.2 FDDI

Fibre Distributed Data Interface (FDDI) provides a 100 Mbit/s data rate. It is expensive, but the high bandwidth and ability to cover distance make it attractive as a backbone technology. It is also used where particular applications need the greater bandwidth. A new version of the protocol on twisted pair, copper distributed data interface (CDDI), promises lower cost access to 100 Mbit/s.

FDDI is a ring protocol. Access to the network is controlled by passing a special frame from machine to machine called a token. The machine with the token is allowed to transmit data for a limited period before passing the token on to the next machine in the ring. Token passing does not place the same geographical constraints on a network that collision detection does and this, along with the use of fibre-optic cabling, is why FDDI networks are good for tying together large sites.

3.5.3 *Token Ring*

Token Ring comes in two speeds, a relatively slow 4 Mbit/s and a faster 16 Mbit/s. It is moderately expensive and runs on shielded twisted pair wiring. Token Ring, as its name suggests, is a ring protocol like FDDI.

3.5.4 *ATM*

Asynchronous Transfer Mode (ATM) is a newly emerging standard developed by the telecommunications industry. There have been proposals to extend its use into local area networking and many wild claims have been made about this technology by its proponents. There are still difficult technical problems to overcome before ATM will be a viable local area networking technology, and it will be a few years before any cost effective solutions are likely to be available.

It is unclear whether this technology is suited to local area networking. ATM is based on switching and, as we will see in the following discussions on network traffic and network design, switching within workgroups can lead to problems of unfairness and high frame loss.

3.6 LAN traffic

LAN traffic tends to be hierarchical, with most traffic flowing between machines that are close together and much less going to remote machines. This pattern reflects the structure of the organisation that uses the network. Most organisations are structured hierarchically, and so is the network traffic.

The increasing popularity of client/server computing has significantly strengthened hierarchical flows of traffic (see Figure 3.8), as well as greatly increasing overall traffic levels.

Typically a department, or workgroup, will have a server that provides shared storage of data. Whenever members of the workgroup need access to the information, it is quickly copied over the network to their computer. They are termed 'clients' of the server. Most of the data tends to flow from the server to the clients. This is fairly intuitive, programs are used, not altered, whole documents read, and only parts changed. It is analogous to the use of a filing cabinet – files are often referenced, but less frequently updated or added.

As well as needing to share information at the workgroup level, organisations often need to share information more widely, and 'global' servers are used that are accessed from many workgroups.

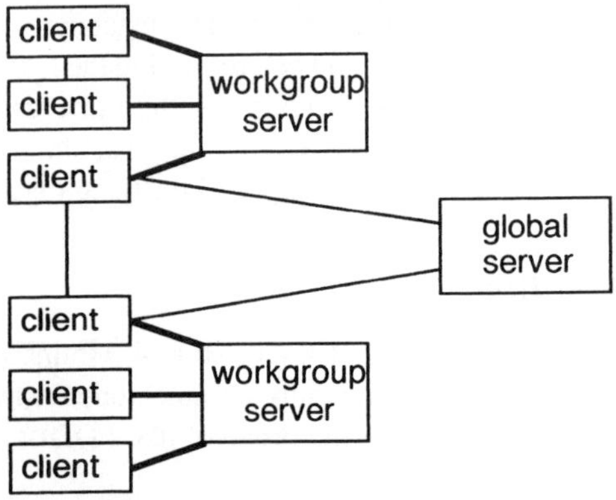

Figure 3.8
Hierarchical flow of traffic.

There is an increasing variety of servers being used. The most prevalent is the file server just discussed, and there are a wide variety of file servers in use. Compute servers provide access to powerful computation or simulation facilities. X-Windows servers (X is a network based graphical user interface) centralise most of the application and leave the client to display the graphics.

The increasing traffic levels, brought about by the use of client/server installations and the growth in network sizes, has become significantly worse as machines have become faster. Typical computer networking speeds have increased to the point where very few machines are needed to saturate a local area network. Careful network design is needed in order to avoid congestion problems.

3.7 Designing a LAN

Let's bring all these ideas together and see how they impact the design of the network. Networks are generally built up hierarchically – machines are connected together to form workgroups, workgroups are connected together within buildings and finally buildings may be connected together within a campus or internationally via a wide area network. We'll go through each of these steps in the following sections.

3.7.1 Workgroups

Repeaters are usually the best choice for connecting machines within a workgroup together. From a traffic management standpoint repeaters provide a number of benefits. The areas connected by repeater provide fair, shared access to all the attached machines. Attaching an instrument anywhere in a workgroup connected by repeaters allows all the traffic to be seen and so allows simple cost effective monitoring of the traffic in the workgroup. Very few frames will be lost in a repeater network, even at very high traffic levels. Low frame loss is important because many workgroup applications show poor reliability and performance if many frames are lost.

Cost is a big issue. In this hierarchical design most of the network interfaces will be in the workgroup so choosing low cost devices such as repeaters is attractive.

Figure 3.9 shows a typical workgroup connected by a number of repeaters. There are a number of clients and a single server within the workgroup.

Fair access to the server is important. As we discussed earlier, most workgroup traffic is between the clients and the workgroup server. The server is the resource that needs to be shared among the clients and so the fairness of access is important to ensure that no clients are denied access. The low latency provided by repeaters can improve the performance of server access. Because most of the traffic involves the server, there is no benefit in partitioning the workgroup, and overall performance is limited by the speed of the server and the basic network speed.

3.7.2 Connecting workgroups

Combining workgroups together with repeaters will work until the overall traffic levels start to get high. It is then time to introduce devices that will separate traffic, reducing the workgroup traffic levels. A good choice is the bridge. Bridges should be added with caution. As soon as we add devices other than repeaters we will see higher frame loss rates and a loss of fairness in accessing the network.

These problems occur because each interface on a bridge (or a router) has only one station's access to each attached network, even though it may have many machines behind it.

In Figure 3.10 a workgroup is split in two with a bridge. If the server is in heavy use then the four clients to the left of the bridge will only get one quarter of the access to the server that the other clients are getting. This unfairness is translated into frame loss when a number of stations attached to one or more interfaces on the bridge send frames to machines connected to another interface. The bridge is forced to store frames, and, if it runs out of memory, to drop them. In the example, if the four clients on the left make requests and the server net-

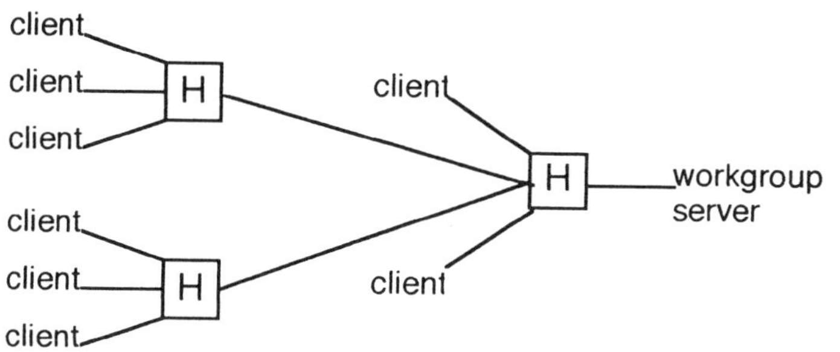

Figure 3.9
A workgroup connected by repeaters (repeater = H).

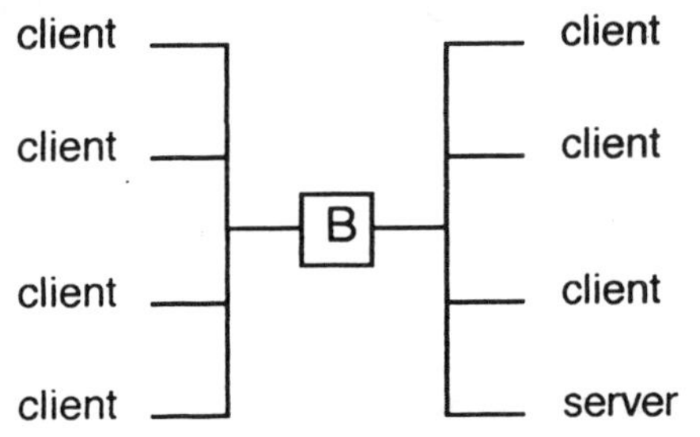

Figure 3.10
A workgroup split by a bridge (bridge = B).

work is busy, it is likely that the bridge will drop some queries. The clients on the right do not suffer this problem. In this example adding a bridge or router has made things worse, reducing access and increasing loss for the clients on the left.

Congestive loss of frames can be a serious problem if the network boundaries don't accurately match the traffic patterns. The following examples should illustrate how some of these problems can occur.

1. File servers are focal points for heavy network activity. As we saw, if the clients are on different bridge ports from the server there can be heavy frame loss.
2. Some protocols (such as transmission control protocol (TCP)) are designed to work efficiently in wide area networks and so are tuned to deal with packet loss, in fact to maximise throughput they push traffic to the level at which there is packet loss. If a connection of this type is running across a bridge or router that is being shared by other less robust LAN protocols they will compete and the LAN protocol can suffer high frame loss and poor performance.

Because of these problems, overpartitioning can be as much of a problem as underpartitioning. It is sometimes worth removing bridges or routers and replacing them with repeaters in order to consolidate workgroups.

Bridges have a number of advantages over routers when connecting workgroups together. Bridges are less expensive than routers. They are very easy to set up, learning what they need from the network traffic. Routers, on the other hand, require considerable effort to set up and complicate the configuration of all the networked machines.

Organisations often change, and these reorganisations are reflected in changing workgroup groupings. Routed networks require administrative information in the routers and attached machines to be changed when the network is changed. Bridges will adapt automatically to the changes.

Another issue is that of dealing with the many different protocols that are often used within the workgroups. Routers need to be set up for each protocol they are to route; they often only support a limited number of protocols, and there are certain protocols that cannot be routed. Bridges on the other hand will deal with all the different protocols without configuration.

There are occasions when the use of a router is appropriate for connecting workgroups. If the workgroups use different media access protocols then a router can be a good way to connect them. It provides the mechanisms to deal with different media access address formats and frame sizes. Hybrid bridge/router devices called translating bridges can also be used to perform this task. They preserve many of the ease of use characteristics of bridges, but they are sophisticated devices and can produce interesting problems. If security within the site is important then the access control capabilities of a router may be appropriate, although using the access control features may impact performance.

Bridges typically have two interfaces. Recently new types of bridge have become popular that have more ports. These can provide good performance and end up costing less than a larger number of two port bridges. They are also very useful for sharing site or global servers.

The traditional way to partition a site is to have each workgroup bridged off from a backbone to which the site servers are attached (see Figure 3.11). This arrangement works well. It does, however, have limitations if the traffic levels on the backbone increase. The backbone is shared by traffic to the servers and by traffic between the workgroups; this could become a bottleneck.

If a multiport bridge is used to replace the backbone (see Figure 3.12) the bottleneck disappears. The bridge does need to be considerably faster than the network in order to provide this improvement.

There is a new type of multiport device emerging that is a hybrid between a bridge and a repeater. Unlike a bridge it starts to transmit the frame as soon as it receives the destination address. While these devices can reduce latency they don't provide the isolation of errors that a bridge provides.

3.7.3 Connecting sites

Connecting sites together involves the use of expensive, relatively low speed, low reliability links. Routers are usually a good choice for connecting sites together (see Figure 3.13). Routers allow redundant links to be built into the net-

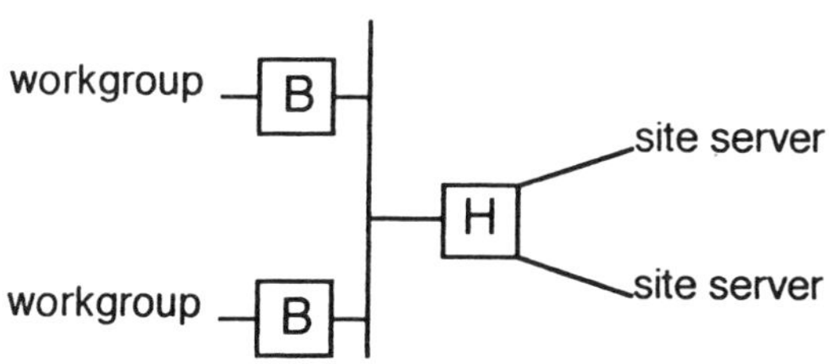

Figure 3.11
Backbone connecting site servers to bridged workgroups (repeater = H, bridge = B).

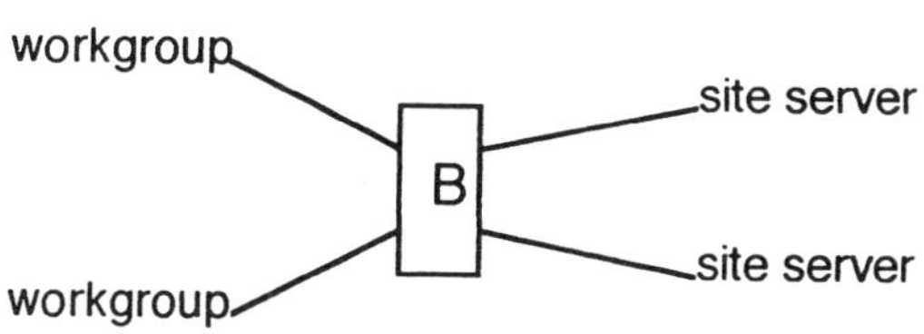

Figure 3.12
Bridge connecting workgroups and site servers (bridge = B).

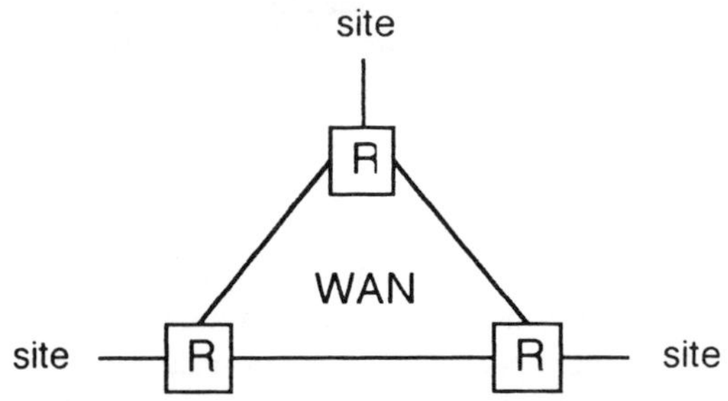

Figure 3.13
Sites connected with routers (router = R).

work and efficiently used. When a link fails the routers will automatically reroute traffic around the failure.

Bridges, running the spanning tree protocol, can also be connected with redundant links. They are not as efficient because under normal conditions they will switch off the redundant links, only using them when there is a failure.

If bridges are used they will forward broadcast and multicast traffic on to the wide area network. This can waste a lot of bandwidth. Routers can limit broadcast traffic to the sites.

These wide area links may also connect into public networks and so pose a security risk. Routers can provide sophisticated filtering capabilities that help eliminate some types of threat.

The basic trade-off between bridges and routers is one of ease of use against better control. It is possible to mix bridges and routers in the wide area network design to achieve a balance between these characteristics.

There is a lot more to wide area network design than has been described here. It is worth getting expert advice about router configuration, tariffs, security and capacity planning before attempting to build a wide area network.

3.7.4 Putting it all together

We have discussed how to connect machines to form workgroups, workgroups to form sites, and connect sites to form an enterprise network. We can now put these ideas together to see what a typical site network might look like.

Figure 3.14 shows a network topology making use of these principles. Each workgroup is connected together by repeaters; the workgroups are separated by bridges. Routers are used to connect to the wide area network and to connect the Ethernet, token ring and FDDI networks together.

A final issue to discuss is that of network reliability. One of the best ways to ensure reliable networking is to choose good quality, reliable components and to check all cabling as it is installed. Ensuring that the connectivity devices are only accessible to authorised personnel helps to prevent unauthorised changes that can lead to problems. These measures should significantly improve network reliability, but they may not be enough if the network is so critical that downtime cannot be tolerated. In this case a careful use of redundancy can help. Some

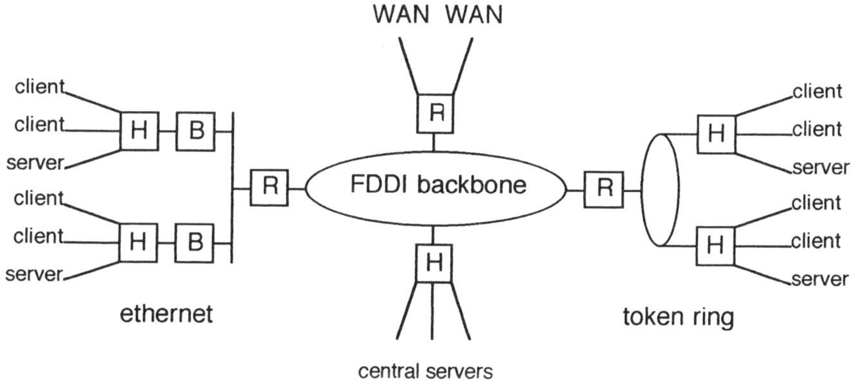

Figure 3.14
Complete site network (repeater = H, bridge = B router = R).

repeaters have provision for backup links, should their primary link fail. Bridges can be connected in a mesh if they support the spanning tree protocol. Routers are designed to operate in mesh networks and so multiple paths can be created between each router. The aim of meshing is to ensure that no single component or cable failure will break connectivity in the network. Often hybrid solutions are appropriate: workgroups will not be meshed, but the backbone and server connections will be.

3.8 Wiring for change

Suppose you are responsible for managing the network inside a large building. Each floor has a number of offices, and each office is connected by twisted pair cables to an equipment room near the stairs. In this example let's consider one of the floors in the building (see Figure 3.15).

Initially the rooms are wired as shown in Figure 3.16, each row of offices is connected to a hub, the two hubs are connected together, and a bridge connects them to the building backbone, running up the stairwell. This works well. It separates the floor's traffic from the building backbone.

There are two different groups working on this floor: the first occupies rooms 1 to 10 and the second rooms 11 to 20. When these groups each install file servers the traffic increases to a point where the network starts to become congested.

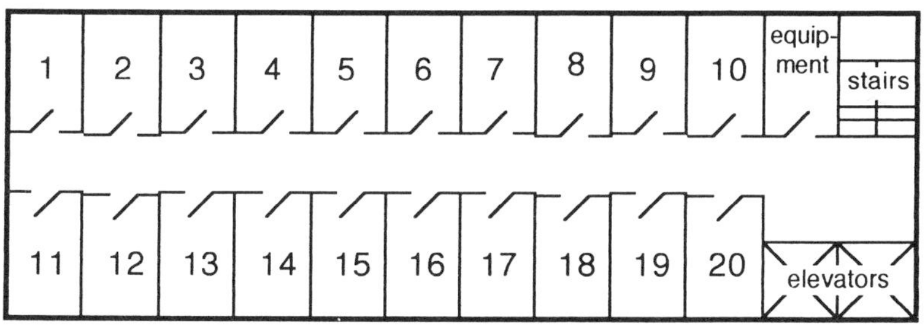

Figure 3.15
Building floor plan.

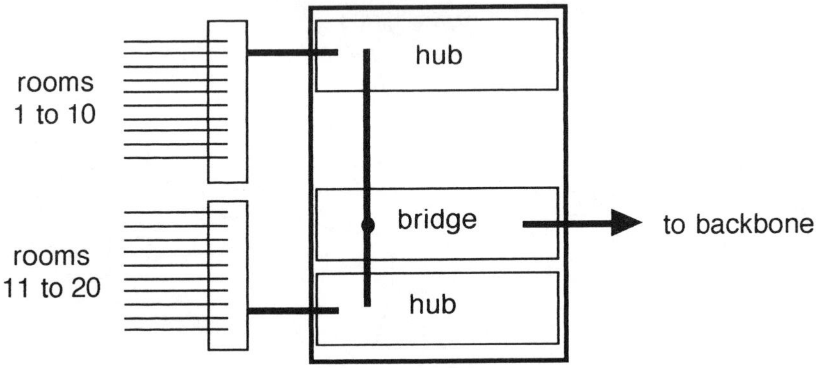

Figure 3.16
Bridging floor from building backbone.

Installing a second bridge (see Figure 3.17) so that the two groups are separated from each other and from the backbone halves the traffic levels on each group's network. In addition one of the groups is working on confidential material and the bridge provides some security for the data they are using, ensuring that it cannot be seen by anyone outside the group.

The one group expands to occupy room number 11 in addition to rooms 1 to 10. This change is easily accommodated by connecting the cable from room 11 to the hub serving rooms 1 to 10 (as shown in Figure 3.18).

Throughout this example the ability to change the wiring from the central equipment room, and the modular equipment installed there, have allowed the network to adapt to changing demands. This style of wiring is termed 'structured wiring'.

What might not have been so obvious from this example are the administrative problems of keeping an up to date record of the network configuration and the applications and groups making use of it. In a perfect world no one would make changes without telling the network manager, but this seldom happens. This is where network management tools come into their own. They allow the

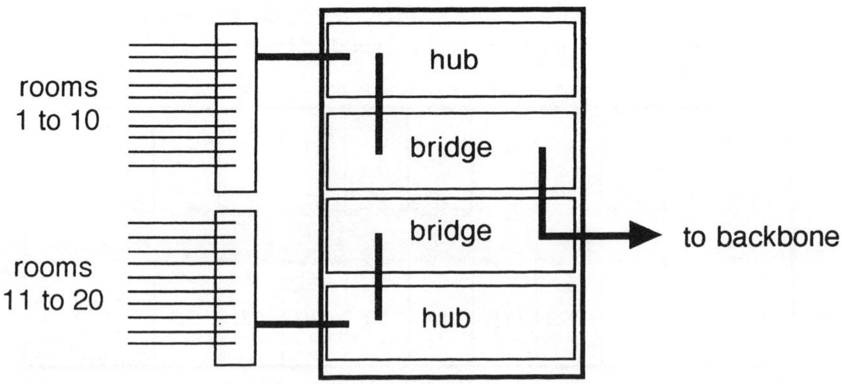

Figure 3.17
Separating workgroups with a bridge.

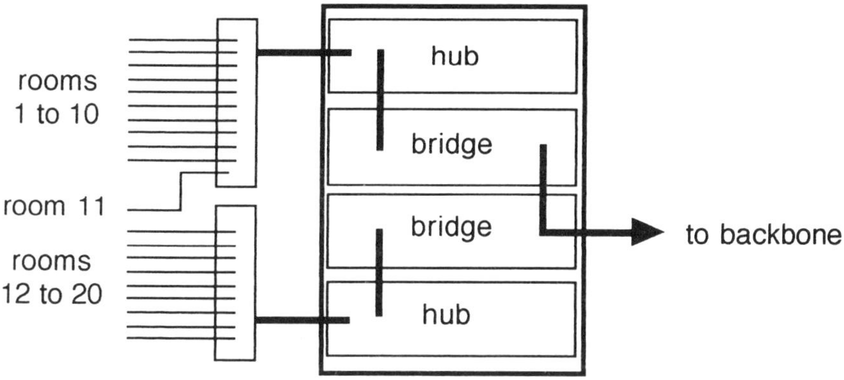

Figure 3.18
Move room 11 between workgroups.

network configuration to be automatically monitored and keep the manager informed of configuration changes. In addition by looking at the traffic on the network it is possible to identify the different groups of users and the applications they use.

3.9 Physical and logical topology

In the structured wiring example we followed the hierarchical model for designing the network (see Figure 3.19).

A common requirement is the desire to place the workgroup servers together in a central location so that they can be centrally administered. This appears to cause a problem because they will now be on the opposite side of the bridge from their clients.

A solution is to run a spur from each workgroup to the central computer room (see Figure 3.20). This way the servers can be centralised while maintaining the advantages of having them 'close' to their clients in a logical sense. This separation between logical and physical topology is important to remember when designing LANs since it often allows competing objectives to be realised at the same time.

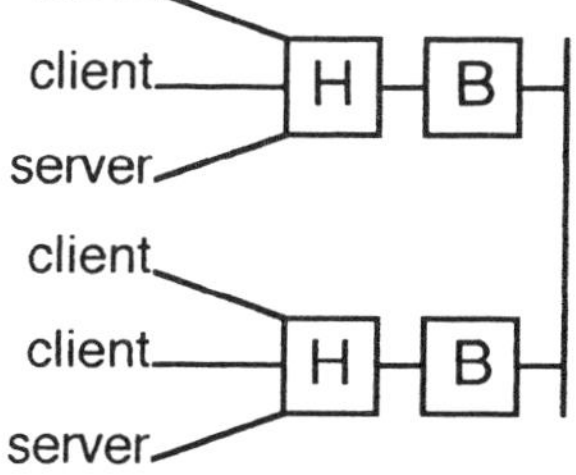

Figure 3.19
Logical view of two bridged workgroups (repeater = H, bridge = B).

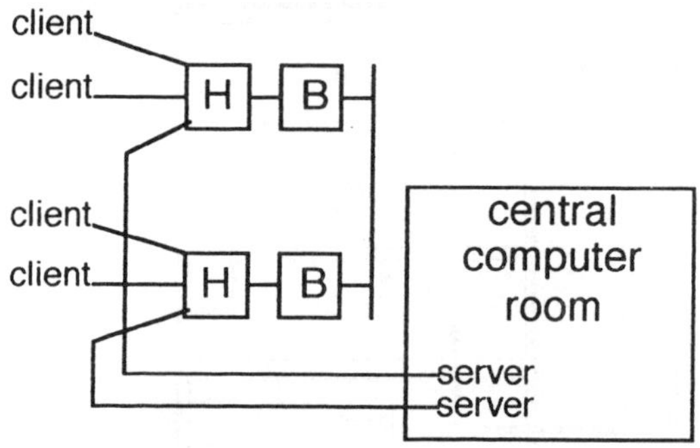

Figure 3.20
Centrally locating work-group servers (repeater = H, bridge = B).

3.10 Family of strategic tools

A number of related tasks need to be performed to provide long term traffic management. These activities and the types of tools needed to support them are best illustrated by example.

The HP EASE applications will be used to illustrate long term traffic management activities and the way they interrelate. Three of the applications are aimed at the long term management of LAN traffic. These are the Report Generator, the Workgroup Analyzer and the History Analyzer. These three tools work together to provide powerful capabilities for detecting emerging traffic problems, identifying possible solutions and planning the changes needed to ensure the continued smooth running of the network.

Typically problems will be identified by the Report Generator. Continuous network-wide monitoring produces a lot of data and finding the useful information can be very difficult. The Report Generator runs every night learning about the normal traffic patterns on the network and identifying unusual behaviour. It also looks for ways in which the network can be altered to improve performance and suggests these changes. The problems that the Report Generator identifies can be analysed in two ways, either by looking at the traffic flows related to the network topology in order to understand topology changes, or by looking at traffic flows over time to understand emerging trends (see Figure 3.21). The Workgroup Analyzer and History Analyzer respectively provide these analysis capabilities. We will look at some of the basic capabilities that each of these tools provides to accomplish these tasks.

3.10.1 Report Generator

The Report Generator runs every night to produce reports automatically for the different networks being monitored (see Figure 3.22). It identifies the sites that need attention and focuses on problem areas and possible solutions. It provides enough information to start a detailed analysis of a problem site. Analysis tools, such as the History and Workgroup Analyzers, need some starting information

Figure 3.21
Long term management applications and tasks.

in order to be useful, at least a basic problem description and its general location. By themselves the analysis tools provide too much detail – they need the reporter to start them off in the right direction.

Each report comprises a number of tables selected from different packages available in the application. Each report specifies a protocol, time of day, and sites on which it is to be run. A problem with many report generators is that they produce very long reports. There may be important information in the reports, but it is tedious to try and find it.

To solve this problem the Report Generator makes use of many of the techniques for highlighting important information described in Section 2.8.

1. A learning mechanism is used which involves watching for changes from day to day. This, in combination with the other techniques, highlights recent changes that might cause problems.

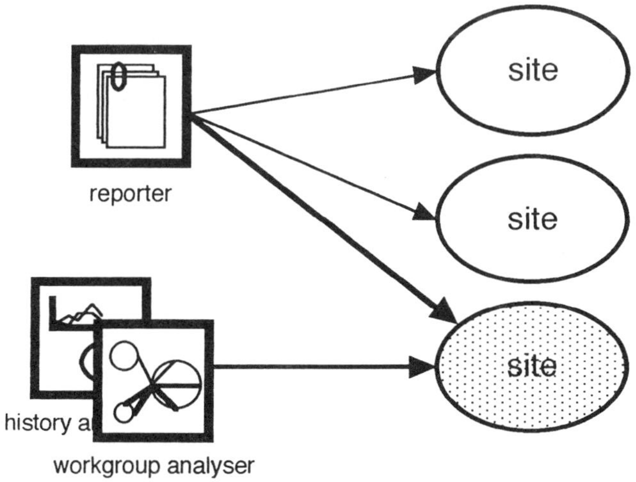

Figure 3.22
Reporter identifies problem site which is then analysed.

2. A number of the tables produced by the Report Generator contain sorted lists of network devices. Some of these tables are used to find the odd one out, looking for machines whose traffic patterns are unusual when compared to the rest. Others are used to identify major contributors to important statistics so that major problems can be fixed first.
3. The Report Generator has tables aimed at controlling and improving network partitioning. Because it runs every day, it only needs to look for small misconfigurations and identify simple configuration changes in order to keep the network well partitioned.

The application of these techniques should become clearer as the functionality of the Report Generator is more fully described in this section and as detailed examples are presented at the end of this chapter.

There are five major packages in the Report Generator covering key aspects of network traffic management.

3.10.1.1 Workgroup package

The workgroup package is concerned with managing client/server networks. The package can discover four main types of entity:

1. Global servers, providing services to clients in different workgroups.
2. Local servers, providing services within a workgroup.
3. Clients, machines making use of a server.
4. Workgroups, combining a local server and its clients.

Identifying these entities involves the use of the technique of looking for small changes (see Section 2.8.5). If we assume that the network is reasonably well partitioned then the local servers can be identified as those servers whose clients are mostly on a single segment. Identifying the local servers allows us to identify the different workgroups. Global servers are easily identified as servers that have clients spread across a number of segments. If the network is very badly partitioned then some initial work will need to be done to improve it before this package will be effective.

Having identified these entities from the traffic patterns the package can produce a number of different types of report. The following tables are available within this package:

1. Workgroup: Client/Server Move Suggestions
2. Workgroup: Segment Splitting Suggestions
3. Workgroup: Top Global Servers (by bytes)
4. Workgroup: Top Global Servers (by frames)
5. Workgroup: Top Global Servers (by number of clients)
6. Workgroup: Top Local Servers (by bytes)
7. Workgroup: Top Local Servers (by frames)
8. Workgroup: Top Local Servers (by number of clients)
9. Workgroup: Top Clients (by bytes)

10. Workgroup: Top Clients (by frames)
11. Workgroup: Top Clients (by number of servers)
12. Workgroup: Top Segment Pairs (by bytes)
13. Workgroup: Top Segment Pairs (by frames)

When a client is on a different segment from that of its local server then it will be suggested that the client be moved to the server's segment. When a local server is on a different segment from most of its clients then it will be suggested that the server, along with any clients on its segment, be moved to the segment with the most clients. Segments that communicate heavily together may be candidates for merging, and segments with more than one workgroup on them are candidates for splitting. Implementing these move suggestions has a number of benefits:

1. Performance is improved by reducing the number of segments that the traffic must cross.
2. Reliability is improved because network failures will no longer affect the workgroup services.
3. Security is improved because workgroup traffic will be kept on the workgroup segment.

This type of analysis can yield meaningless results if used on protocols that are not being used in a strongly client/server architecture. The best results are obtained for file sharing protocols such as NFS (Network File System), diskless and IPX (Internet Packet eXchange protocol), because file sharing, as well as being a client/server application, is one of the most bandwidth-intensive and delay-sensitive classes of traffic in the local area network.

Machines may run many different protocols and have different relationships within each protocol. This means that you can get contradictory suggestions if you run this analysis on different protocols. It is then necessary to decide which service is the most important and should be optimised.

It is worth remembering that a server is software running on a machine and that moves can be realised by replicating or moving services from one machine to another. Also there may be many servers offering the same service on the network and so rather than moving a client to its server it could be better to make it a client of another server.

If structured wiring is being used it is often possible to make 'moves' simply by changing connections on a patch panel.

3.10.1.2 Traffic package

The traffic package is primarily concerned with finding extremes (see Section 2.8.2). Problems usually show up as one form of extreme behaviour or another.

The following tables are included within this package:

1. Traffic: Protocol Breakdown Summary
2. Traffic: Top Destinations of Bytes

3. Traffic: Top Destinations of Frames
4. Traffic: Top Node Pairs (by bytes)
5. Traffic: Top Node Pairs (by frames)
6. Traffic: Top Nodes (by number of destinations)
7. Traffic: Top Nodes (by number of sources)
8. Traffic: Top Sources of Bytes
9. Traffic: Top Sources of Frames
10. Traffic: Top Sources of Broadcasts
11. Traffic: Top Sources of Multicasts
12. Traffic: Unknown Protocols

These tables are particularly powerful when used in conjunction with the 'learning' option. This allows a large number of tables to be included in the report, but for short reports showing changes to be produced.

3.10.1.3 Segment-statistics package

Segment statistics allow overloaded segments to be identified so that corrective actions can be taken, possibly by splitting the segment using the 'Workgroup: Segment Splitting Suggestions' table. Many types of problem to do with the physical wiring will also show up as high error rates in the segment error statistics.

The following table is included in the package:

1. Segment-Statistics: Segment Statistics Totals

3.10.1.4 Security package

Looking at the activity from nodes outside the management area can indicate security problems. Unusual activity could indicate unauthorised access to site machines. The effectiveness of this package can be improved by creating reports for particular protocols, for example login activity from remote sites tends to be more threatening than electronic mail. It also helps to use the 'learning' option with security reports, so that new activity is quickly identified.

The following tables are included in the package:

1. Security: Outside Nodes (sorted by bytes received)
2. Security: Outside Nodes (sorted by frames received)
3. Security: Outside Nodes (sorted by no. of connections)

3.10.1.5 Troubleshooting package

This package contains tables that deal with well-known types of problem. The following tables are included in this package:

1. Troubleshooting: Duplicate IP Addresses
2. Troubleshooting: Top Error Sources

A duplicate IP address occurs when more than one host has been configured to use the same IP address. This may mean that neither host can reliably communicate. Machines generating high levels of errors may have faulty LAN cards.

3.10.2 Workgroup Analyzer

The Workgroup Analyzer allows time periods, protocols and sites to be selected as the basis of queries. In response to a query it will produce a graphical view of the traffic patterns as they relate to the site topology (see Figure 3.23).

The view shown in Figure 3.24 consists of a number of circles, one for each segment being monitored. Each dot on the circle represents a computer attached to the segment. Lines connecting the dots together represent traffic between the machines and the width of the lines represents the volume of traffic. The Workgroup Analyzer provides many functions that allow this display to be controlled. In the diagram we can see that some of the machines have their names showing. It is apparent that the machines 'wol', 'everest' and 'krakatoa' are the focus of considerable activity and are probably servers.

The view provides considerable control over what is displayed. Functions such as selecting nodes, zooming, labelling and locating aim to make it easy to explore and analyse problem areas.

This type of display is very useful for understanding recommendations from the Report Generator and for visually exploring the relationships between machines. The examples at the end of this chapter should help to illustrate the use of this application.

The Workgroup Analyzer is a good example of a tool that provides a network level view (see Section 2.8.6). Combining traffic information from across the entire site and presenting it in a simple single view that focuses on the network partitions greatly simplifies the analysis of the traffic patterns.

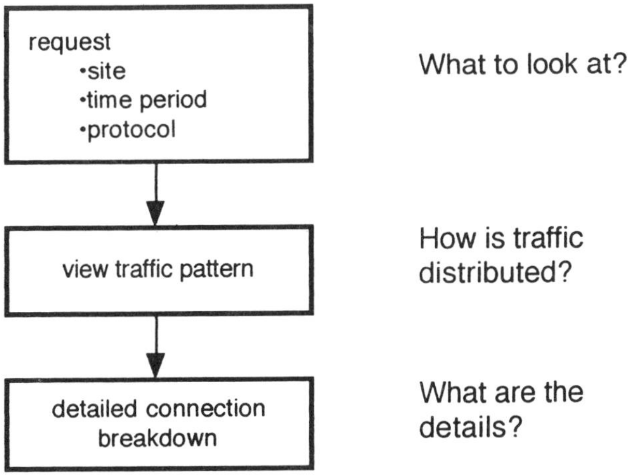

Figure 3.23
Traffic pattern analysis activities.

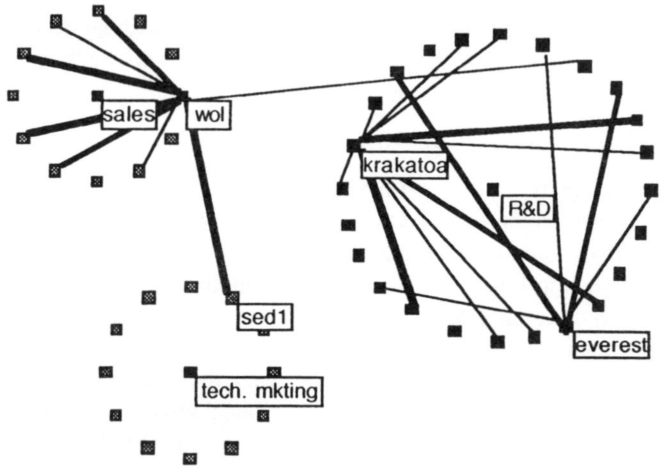

Figure 3.24
Typical traffic view.

3.10.3 History Analyzer

The History Analyzer supports a number of queries that allow traffic information to be plotted as a function of time.

Many network activities show periodic behaviour. Interactive traffic tends to reflect the working day, building up during the morning, dipping for lunch and then finally dying out in the late afternoon. There is often a lot of activity during the night as systems are automatically backed up.

As well as being useful for understanding periodic behaviour, the history analyser can be used to look at growth of traffic and to assess the significance of recent network loads. There is no point in responding to a situation that was a one-off and is not likely to occur again. On the other hand if a certain load has been growing gradually over the past few weeks it may be sensible to do something about it.

The History Analyzer is structured to facilitate exploration of data. Results are kept in a workspace so that they can be compared. Queries associated with each result can be recalled and modified (see Figure 3.25), making it easy to repeat a particular analysis for a different protocol or over a different time period.

The graphical queries supported by the History Analyzer include:

1. Address mappings
2. Network traffic level
3. Top talkers
4. Top error sources
5. Top broadcasters
6. Top service users
7. Top service providers
8. Utilisation on segment

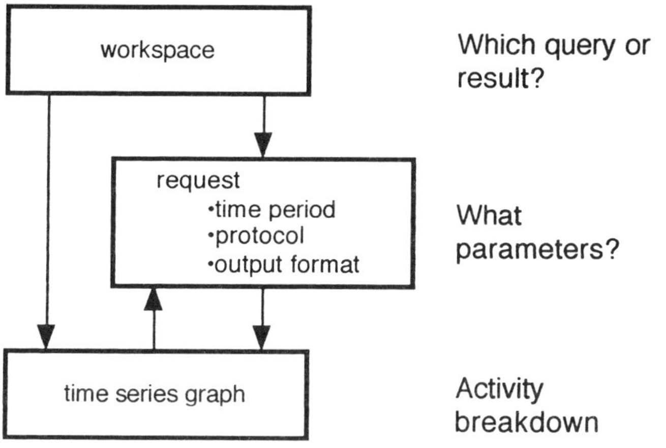

Figure 3.25 Traffic history analysis activities.

9. Protocol usage on segment
10. Errors on segment
11. Service breakdown for address
12. Error breakdown for address
13. Service traffic level

As well as providing graphical queries, a number of command line queries are provided that can be used in custom scripts or importing data into statistics, reporting, billing or spreadsheet applications. These command line queries include:

easeaddrmap	returning address mappings
easedata	returning the time period for which data is available
easeerrors	returning the top error sources
easesegcount	returning segment statistics
easesegmap	returning a description of each segment
easetraffic	returning traffic matrices
easecost	a simple billing script

The History Analyzer does not provide forecasting tools. In general, past traffic behaviour is a poor predictor of future growth. Traffic patterns tend to show periods of stability separated by rapid change as changes are made to the network. Forecasting is best done by looking at future plans for application deployment and equipment purchase rather than by looking at traffic.

One final but important use of the History Analyzer is to make use of the history as an audit trail. For example, suppose that there have been problems with unauthorised accesses to an important server. If the times of these accesses are known, the History Analyzer can be used to identify a list of likely culprits by finding out who was connected to the server at those times.

3.11 Management checklist

Long term management of the network needs to be viewed as a process. While the traffic management tools may help to automate parts of this process most of it is organisational and involves human activity. This section attempts to describe the daily and monthly management process through the creation of checklists that can be used as the basis of defining a management strategy.

The daily and monthly checklists split activities into two distinct classes: the daily activities that are aimed at ensuring that the network is operating well and that highlight any emerging problems early enough so that action can be taken, and the monthly activities that anticipate and assess changing demand and ensure that the network is grown and changed so that it can provide trouble free service.

These checklists only apply to traffic management. A network manager is likely to have much broader responsibilities and they should also be incorporated into the daily and monthly routine.

These checks are aimed not only at finding problems, but also at confirming that the network is working properly and providing the information needed in order continually to improve it.

3.11.1 Daily checks

1. Is the network congested? Monitor segment utilisations, frame rates and bridge and router packet loss rates in order to detect congestion and identify congested devices.
2. Is the network failing? Monitor error rates on all cables to find faulty cables and LAN interfaces. Often failures will occur gradually making it possible to correct them before they become serious.
3. Is there pollution? Certain types of activity and protocol waste network resources and their levels should be controlled. Unnecessary broadcast or multicast traffic should be limited and protocols which create periodic information messages should have sensible timeout values or if possible be removed.
4. What has changed? Monitor and control the arrival of new traffic sources on the network. Make sure that addresses are properly assigned and watch out for addressing problems such as duplicate IP addresses and incorrect subnet masks. Problems can arise when new protocols, hardware, software or software versions are installed.
5. Are servers overloaded? Large loads on servers can cause serious problems and may be caused by excessive activity by one of the clients. This type of problem can be mistaken for a problem with the network, so it is worth monitoring server traffic. Monitoring network traffic to servers may be the only way to solve these problems because many servers do not have good monitoring tools.
6. Are machines secure? Overall security for corporate data and resources in a networked environment is a large topic and well outside the scope of this book. Where traffic management systems can be helpful is in recording the movement of data in the network and identifying suspicious activity.

3.11.2 Monthly checks

1. Are users satisfied? Finding out how users feel abut network services and what their future plans are is important for planning the deployment of new services and the provision of training and information to users. Informed users create far fewer problems.
2. What changes are planned that are likely to affect traffic? These changes could involve the movement of people, the purchase of new equipment or the installation of new applications and services.
3. Is the network well partitioned? Are there machines that should be moved or segments that should be split?
4. Is there sufficient network capacity? It may be that traffic is growing to a point where even good partitioning will not be sufficient. In this case plans need to be made to migrate to higher speed networking technologies.
5. Is scheduled traffic correctly timed? Many types of network traffic, such as system backup, occur at predefined times. This type of traffic can place a significant load on the network and should be scheduled for off-peak periods such as nighttime or weekends.
6. What should my billing strategy be? Networks are expensive, shared resources, and one way of informing users of the costs and of modifying their behaviour is to charge for network use. Objectives of billing strategies might be to reduce peak traffic by encouraging the use of off-peak times. Billing policies can be used to prioritise network usage, penalising non-critical use of the network during peak times. It is important to keep in mind the wider benefits of having a network: overzealous charging can discourage the free flow of information that makes employees productive. Care should be taken not to create a bureaucracy that is more expensive to administer than the savings it makes in network resources.

The traffic management tools described earlier in this chapter support many of the activities identified in these checklists. The following examples demonstrate the application of the management strategies.

3.12 Examples

The examples presented in this section illustrate the way in which the long term management strategy and tools can provide effective control of network traffic. They also demonstrate the types of 'story' that can be used when designing management tools, and teaching about their use (see Section 2.8.1).

3.12.1 Moving clients

One morning we see the following table in a report from the Report Generator:

```
Workgroup: Client Move Suggestions
---------------------------------
Managed segments only
```

node	server	from segment	to segment
*sbear	wol	R&D	sales
&sedl	wol	tech. mkting	sales
*jharris	tachy	tech. mkting	personnel
*shayes	basil	facilities	shipping

This tells us that two of the clients, machines named 'sbear' and 'sedl', of the server named 'wol' are in the wrong places. 'sbear' should be moved from segment 'R&D' to segment 'sales' and 'sedl' should be moved from segment 'techn. mkting' to 'sales'.

The same report contains another table:

```
Workgroup: Top Local Servers (by number of clients)
---------------------------------------------------
Managed segments only
```

local server	no. clients	server frames in/out %	server byes in/out %	top clients (by frames)
*netmanz	15	25.1	11.3	cgoh pallen rbrown
*wol	13	3.1	2.2	sedl dcoleman pharry
*mcgrew	11	3.1	1.6	mbeech jbruten eccleso
*basil	9	1.2	0.635	rhull idickins shayes
*hplfugue	8	14.8	5.4	msyrett nderret jmanle

We see from this that 'wol' is the second largest server (by number of clients) and that 'sed1' is its major client (by number of frames). This makes a good case for at least moving 'sed1'.

The next thing to do is to examine this situation using the Workgroup Analyzer (see Figure 3.26). It is clear that most of the server's clients are on the

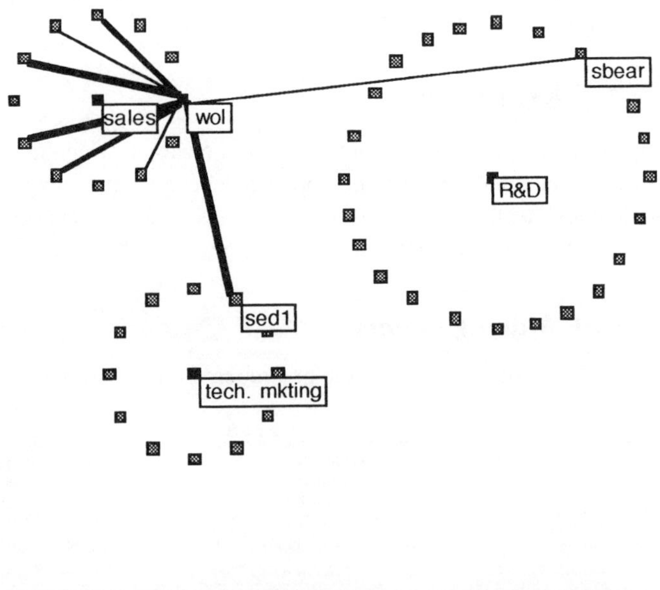

Figure 3.26
Two misplaced clients.

'sales' segment along with the server. 'sedl' and sbear' would clearly be better off on the 'sales' segment, or possibly attached to other servers on their current segments.

3.12.2 *Moving a server*

As well as suggesting moves for clients, the Report Generator can identify misplaced servers. Suppose we get the following report:

```
Workgroup: Move Suggestions For Server: mktsrvl.hpl.hp.com
----------------------------------------------------------
Managed segments only
```

node	server	from segment	to segment
mktsrvl	SERVER	R&D	tech. mkting
vecgr	mktsrvl	R&D	tech. mkting

Taking a look at this situation using the Workgroup Analyzer (see Figure 3.27), we see that the server, 'mktsrvl', has one client, 'vecgr', on its segment. Most of the clients are on the 'tech. mkting' segment and so it makes sense to move the server and its one client to join the others. This will significantly reduce inter-segment traffic and improve the performance of server access. As well as using this qualitative information we can use the Workgroup Analyzer to obtain a detailed profile of the server, 'mktsrvl', simply by pointing at the server.

The profile in Figure 3.28 clearly shows the different services, or protocols, making use of the server (for the User Datagram Protocol (UDP)). It is clear that well over half of the server's activity is due to remote disk access using NFS (Network File System). The activity of each client is profiled and 'vecsp' is identified as the top client. An interesting point to notice is that most data flows from the server to the clients. This is typical of file server access: clients usually read but don't alter data.

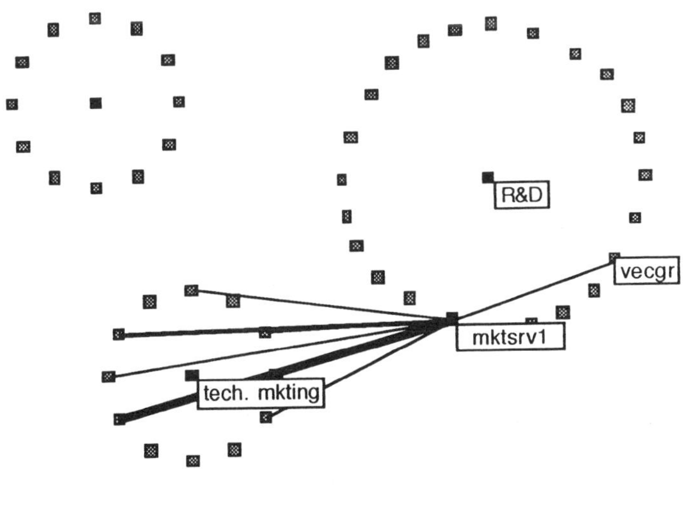

Figure 3.27
Misplaced server.

Badly placed servers can cause major congestion problems on the network. In this case the site was having severe congestion problems on its Ethernet backbone which was running at 90% utilisation. Plans were in place for an upgrade to a 100 Mbit/s FDDI backbone. When only four poorly placed servers were moved the backbone utilisation was reduced to 20%. Performance and reliability were improved and the costly and disruptive upgrade avoided.

3.12.3 Splitting a segment

We get the following report from the Report Generator:

```
Workgroup: Segment Splitting Suggestion For Segment: R&D
-------------------------------------------------------
Managed segments only
```

segment	major workgroup		other nodes	
*R&D	xtmobile	sjohnsto	sbear	everest
	fferrari	maunkea	fredrick	mvocale
	kilauea	helka	meve	newdawn
	fbenussi	krakatoa	sjubb	lynch
	rcastle	mlawton	imoreau	vecgjp
			tgardner	etna
			vecci	rmorassi

This suggests how we can split the 'R&D' segment in order to separate the major workgroup. Looking at this situation with the Workgroup Analyzer we see the situation shown in Figure 3.29.

The group to be split off is easily identified as the machines connected to the server 'krakatoa'. The majority of the rest of the machines are connected to the server 'everest'. These two loosely coupled workgroups could usefully be split if the traffic levels warrant it.

We can use the History Analyzer to take a look at the traffic levels on 'R&D' segment to see if it is worth splitting. Figure 3.30 shows the last five working days. The traffic peaks during the middle of the day with a small dip at lunch time. There is another smaller peak at night when the systems are backed up. Utilisation is very high during the busy periods, reaching 90%. It would make a lot of sense to split this segment using a bridge.

3.12.4 Security alert

One type of security threat is from unauthorised outside access to local machines. Confidential information can be stolen or important machines vandalised. A traffic management system can provide a useful audit trail.

For example, we have set up a daily report to look at all external access to site machines. In a typical day hundreds of different machines may be legitimately accessing the site, so we have set up the report to identify only additions to the normal pattern of traffic. One morning we receive the following report.

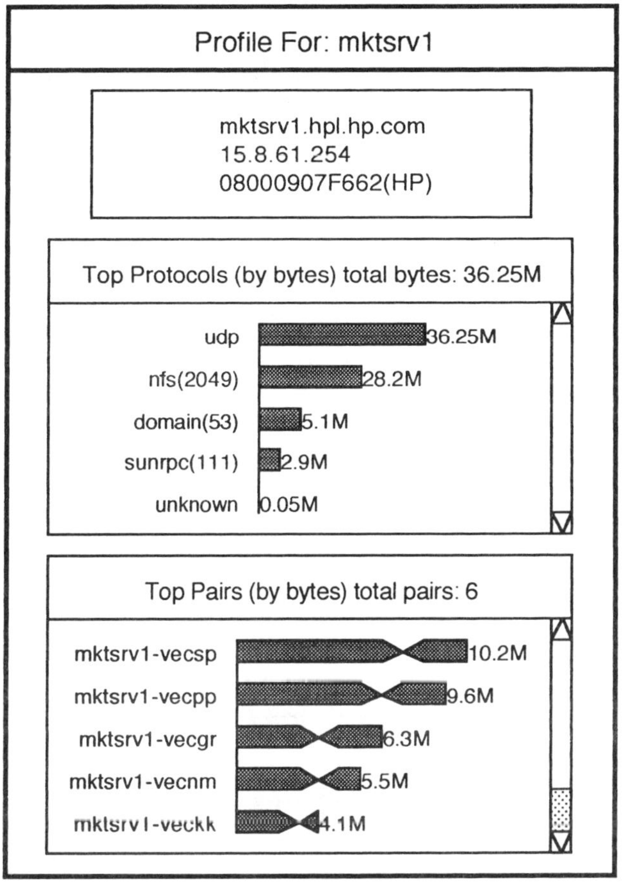

Figure 3.28
Detailed profile of server activity.

```
Security: Outside Nodes (sorted by no. bytes)
----------------------------------------------
Outside connections only
New entries only
```

node	bytes in	frames in	no. peers	top peers (frames)
*ahacker	18.56M	37.1K	1	appsrv
*mailsrv	494.2K	1.2K	14	audrey otter dawn

The second entry looks like a moderate sized mail message sent to a few machines on site from a remote mail server. The first entry on the other hand is worth investigating. It involves a large amount of data, 18.56 Mbytes, being taken from an important site server, 'appsrv'. The suspected culprit is the machine 'ahacker'. The next thing we need to know are the times that 'ahacker' has been accessing our systems and which other systems have been accessed. As well as machines that have been directly accessed, there may have been machine hopping in which one machine is used to get to others. We start by using the

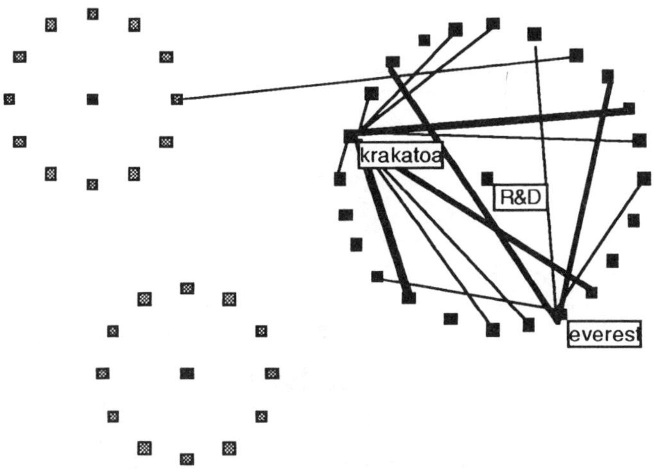

Figure 3.29
Segment with two work-groups.

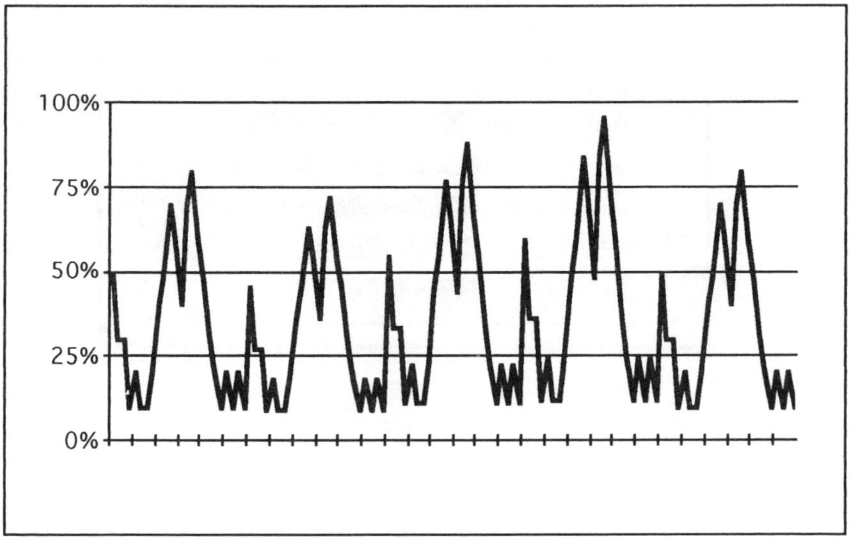

Figure 3.30
Utilisation of R&D segment over five days.

History Analyzer to find the top sources of traffic destined to 'ahacker' over the previous fortnight, broken down by day (see Figure 3.31).

This graph shows that the activity only started in the last day, 17 April. It also shows us that the only machine directly accessed was 'appsrv'. We then take a detailed hourly view (see Figure 3.32).

The activity happened during a four hour period between 2am and 6am. If 'appsrv' is being used as a stepping stone to access other machines on site then we should be able to spot this by looking at the traffic to 'appsrv' during this period (see Figure 3.33).

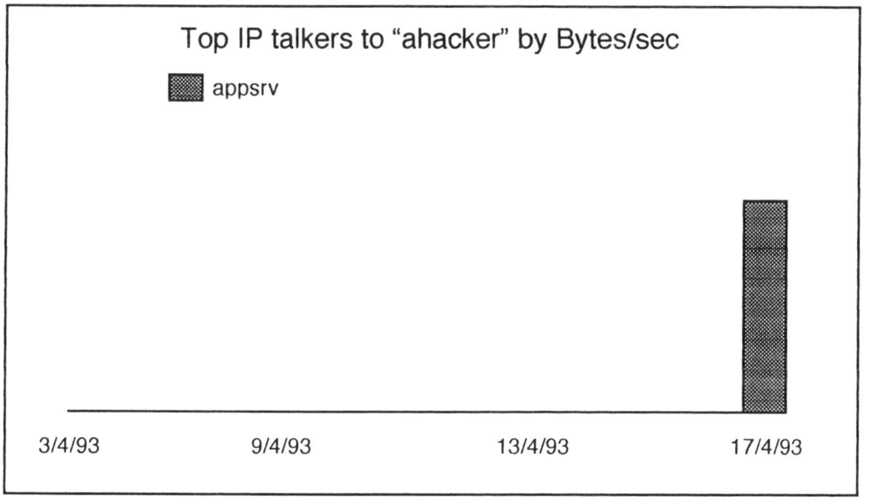

Figure 3.31
Machines communicating with 'ahacker' over two week period.

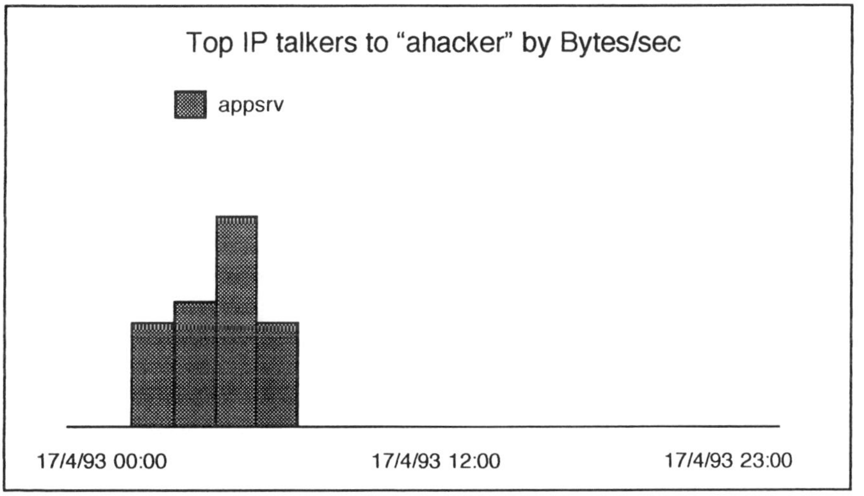

Figure 3.32
Machines communicating with 'ahacker' over 24 hours.

We see that a number of different machines have sent data to 'appsrv'. Interestingly the activity of 'mktsrvl' correlates closely with the traffic going out to 'ahacker'. It seems very likely that information was removed from 'mktsrvl' via 'appsrv'. By looking at the accounting logs on the two machines we get more detailed information on the identity of the hacker, the user accounts used to access the machines, the information that was removed and the security hole used to access the network.

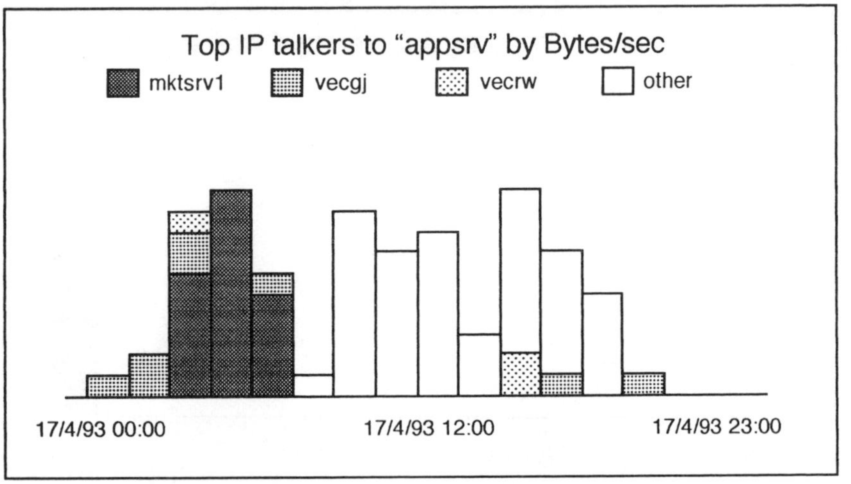

Figure 3.33
Machines communicating with 'appsrv' during 24 hour period.

3.12.5 Speeding up a server

A file server, 'mktsrvl' is behaving sluggishly. One possibility might be that a client is excessively loading the server. Unfortunately there are no performance tools available on the server to identify whether or not this is the case. It is not feasible to examine the fifty clients to find out which one is causing the problem. Since access to the server is via the network we should be able to identify the active clients from the traffic they send to the server. We can use the History Analyzer to look at the top clients accessing 'mktsrvl' (see Figure 3.34).

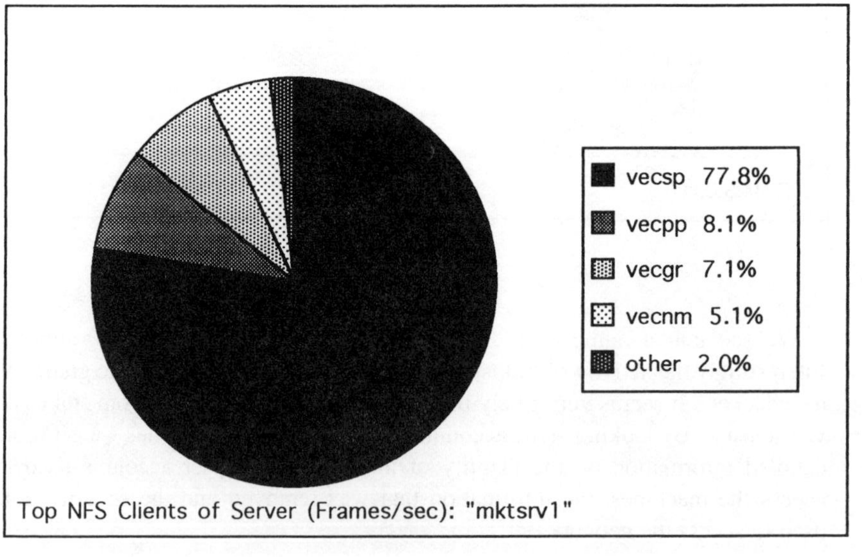

Figure 3.34
Activity of clients of server 'mktsrvl'.

One machine, 'vecsp', clearly stands out as generating more than twice as many requests as all the other clients put together. Further investigation reveals a little used machine running an old backup script that is trying to back up the file server in addition to its own file system. Correction of this script eliminates the problem.

3.12.6 *Finding misconfigured machines*

Connections on a network typically involve a mutual exchange of information. The following report looks at the balance between the number of destinations a machine sends traffic to, and the number of machines that send traffic to it. We expect these numbers to be balanced.

```
Traffic: Top Nodes (by number of sources)
-----------------------------------------
```

node	no. sources	no. destinations	frames out %	bytes out %	top sources of frames
*vecgc	317	6	1.2	0.3	cgoh pallen
*hole	297	299	2.2	3.2	otter slewis
*toad	146	151	1.6	1.1	jmoreau afarm
*netmanx	84	92	0.63	0.74	jjedwab nadin
*pphaal	73	99	5.4	7.8	otter hole

What is interesting is that 'vecgc' receives traffic from 317 other machines, but only sends traffic to 6 machines. This type of traffic generally indicates a configuration problem in which an inappropriate request is broadcast on the network and is answered by a storm of replies. Because all the replies are sent at once they can cause high levels of congestion.

We can take a closer look at the problem using the Workgroup Analyzer (see Figure 3.35).

We clearly see that most machines on the site are sending traffic to 'vecgc'. The 'unmonitored' segment is used to group all addresses that don't belong to machines on monitored segments. Broadcast addresses end up here because they do not refer to individual machines. We can see that 'vecgc' is using the IP (Internet Protocol) broadcast address '15.255.255.255'. This is not the correct broadcast address for this network. The problem is solved by correctly setting vecgc's subnet mask to '255.255.248.0'. The subnet mask is used in IP so that a machine can correctly identify the network and node parts of addresses. Correcting the subnet mask causes vecgc to use the correct broadcast address for this site, '15.8.63.255'.

At this point we may wonder if 'vecgc' was the only machine with this problem. The Workgroup Analyzer can easily show us any other machines using the wrong broadcast address (see Figure 3.36). We can immediately see that 'vecrw' and 'vecsp' are also misconfigured and correct them as well.

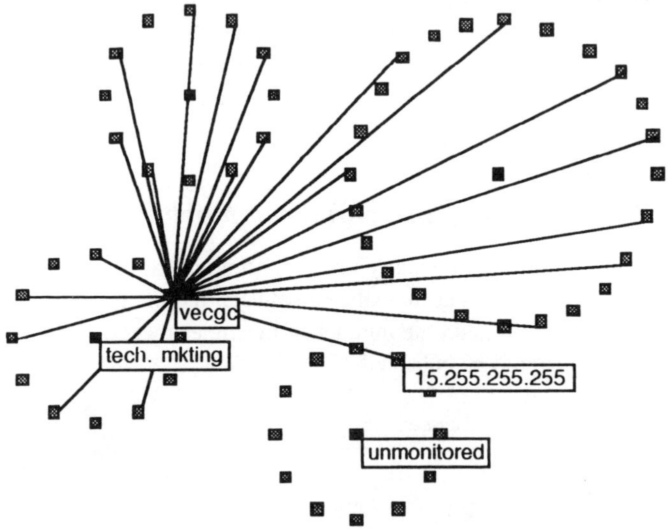

Figure 3.35
View of activity of 'vecgc'.

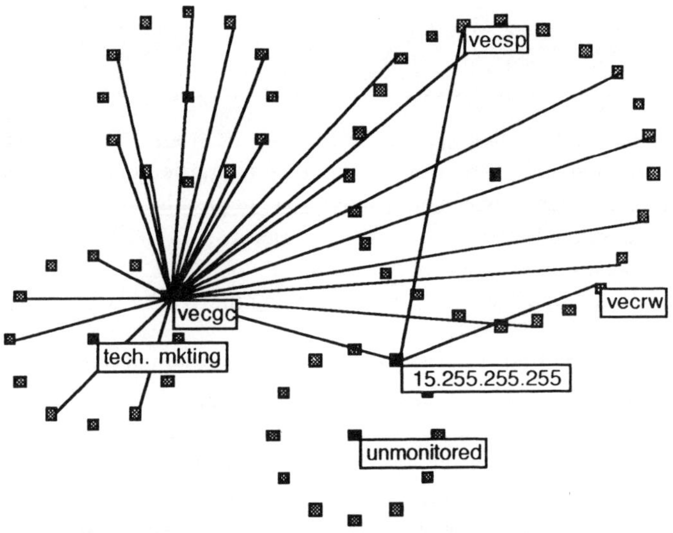

Figure 3.36
Other machines using incorrect broadcast.

3.12.7 Managing broadcast levels

Monitoring the level and sources of broadcasts is very important. Broadcasts are received and processed by all machines attached to the network. If the level of broadcasts is high this unnecessary processing can significantly reduce the performance of machines and in extreme cases, during a broadcast 'storm', bring all machines to a halt. In addition to the load on attached machines broadcasts are forwarded by bridges and so will use bandwidth on a number of segments.

Routine reports should identify the machines generating the most broadcasts, and where possible the levels of broadcasts from these machines should be reduced.

```
Traffic: Top Sources of Broadcasts
----------------------------------
Only broadcast traffic considered
```

node	frames out %	bytes out %
*netmanx	40.32	45.1
*brc-gw	10.1	17.8
*isc-gw	9.1	16.3
*otter	2.2	3.5
*toad	1.3	1.2

This report identifies 'netmanx' as the source of 40% of the broadcasts on the network. Further investigation reveals that they are being caused by a network management application that periodically polls machines to see whether or not they are available. Increasing the polling interval significantly reduced the overall level of broadcasts.

3.12.8 *Finding a faulty LAN interface*

The level of errors on the network should be monitored. Many problems with wiring, repeaters or network adapters occur slowly and show up as increased error rates before they fail completely. By continually monitoring errors these problems can be fixed before they become serious.

Suppose we see the following table in a report.

```
Troubleshooting: Top Error Sources
----------------------------------
```

source address	no. error frames	segment
080009259BE1	12420	sales
08000925BDAB	142	tech. mkting
08000925DBA7	131	R&D
08000925BDA1	22	R&D
0800092742DC	13	sales

The table identifies the machine with address '080009259BE1' as having a significant problem with errors. Because most people will not be familiar with the MAC address of each machine, the Report Generator includes an address table containing other addresses and names associated with each machine in the report.

```
Node Address Mappings
---------------------
```

node	segment	address type	address	other info
sbear	R&D	mac	08000925BDA7	mfg: HP
pharry	sales	mac	080009259BE1	mfg: HP
vecgr	R&D	mac	08000925BDA1	mfg: HP
dcoleman	sales	mac	0800092742DC	mfg: HP
sedl	tech.mkting	mac	08000925BDAB	mfg: HP

We see from the table that the faulty interface belongs to node 'pharry'. The node Media Access Unit (MAU) was replaced and its error rate reduced to zero.

4 Short term management

The long term management of the network should ensure that the network has enough capacity to cope with expected demand and that policies are laid down about the expected levels of traffic. Short term management is aimed at detecting and solving problems that occur because of abnormal or unpredicted behaviour of the network or of unexpected demands being placed on it.

An important element of short term traffic management is the management of congestion. This involves three main activities: detecting that a resource is becoming congested, breaking down the load on that resource so as to identify the cause of the overload and finally taking action to reduce the load to an acceptable level (see Figure 4.1). This may sound simple, but there may be many hundreds of devices on the network, any one of which can become overloaded for a variety of reasons.

4.1 Traffic monitoring

It may seem simplistic just looking for congested devices when the problems that users see relate to connections through multiple devices in the network. Luckily congestion on a path is generally due to a single overloaded 'bottleneck' in the path so that path congestion shows up as congestion of the bottleneck device.

A first step in solving this problem is to recognise that we are primarily interested in finding extremes. We can compare the load on the different parts of the network and see which parts are exceptionally loaded; once we have found an

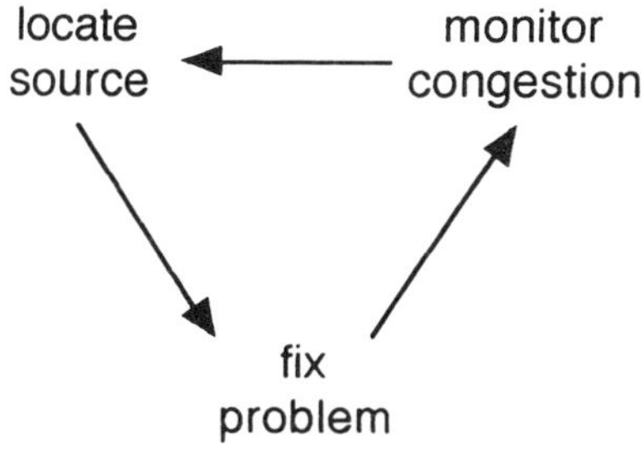

Figure 4.1
Operational management process.

overloaded element we simply need to identify the largest contributors to its load. If we can identify the most congested device and find its largest load, then we have come a long way to solving the problem of congestion monitoring (see Sections 2.8.2 and 2.8.3).

To show how a systematic application of these techniques can result in effective management tools and procedures we can use an example of a tool designed to manage traffic problems with segments on a local area network.

4.1.1 Resource Manager

Typical network management map applications provide information about the status of devices on the network, showing any failed devices in red. They also provide an interface to managed hubs, bridges and routers that allows them to be monitored and controlled.

Detecting traffic problems and identifying their source requires another type of tool. Once the source of a congestion problem has been identified the map tool plays an important role in providing access to the administrative information and controls needed to fix the problem (see Figure 4.2). We will be taking a closer look at these control functions in Section 4.2.

A good traffic monitoring tool should be easy to use and provide a simple path to identifying the source of the problem. When problems occur any time wasted trying to work out what to do next or to remember how to use the tool is additional time during which the network may be unusable. Early detection of problems also helps to buy time so that they can be solved before causing serious disruption.

The Resource Manager simplifies the task of traffic monitoring by explicitly supporting the sequence of actions needed to deal with a traffic problem (see Figure 4.3). The top level view provides a single display that shows whether or not there are traffic problems anywhere in the network. If there is a problem it

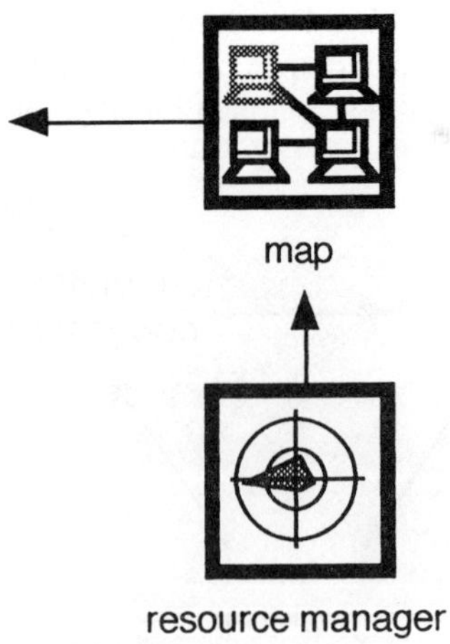

Figure 4.2
Short term management applications and tasks.

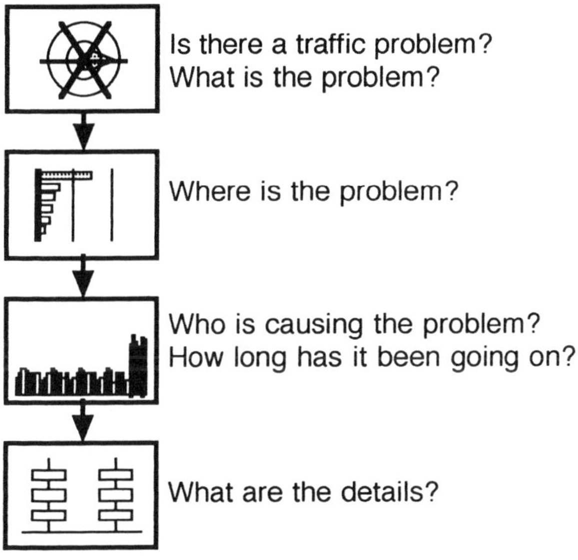

Figure 4.3
Locating congestion.

identifies the type of problem. A click of a button brings up a graph showing where the problem is in the network. A further click identifies the source of the problem. At this point all the details needed to take action can be displayed.

To set up the Resource Manager a policy needs to be established determining the acceptable levels of traffic, broadcasts and errors on any segment. This policy is expressed graphically by drawing a template describing the ranges of values that are good, marginal or critical for each of the key segment statistics (see Figure 4.4).

This policy allows the Resource Manager to combine information from each of the segments it is monitoring in order to produce a single high level view of the state of traffic on the network.

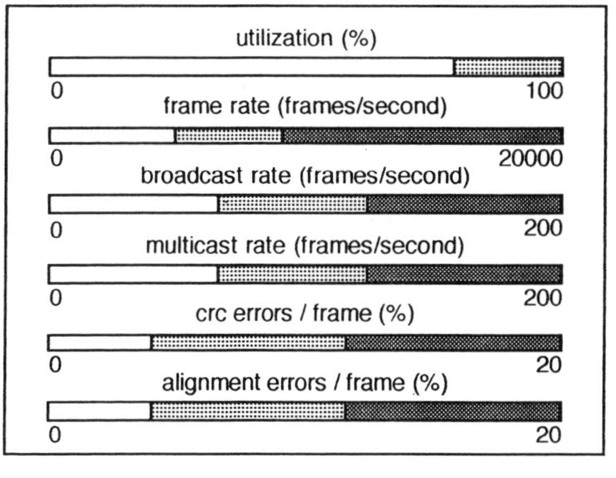

Figure 4.4
Setting policy.

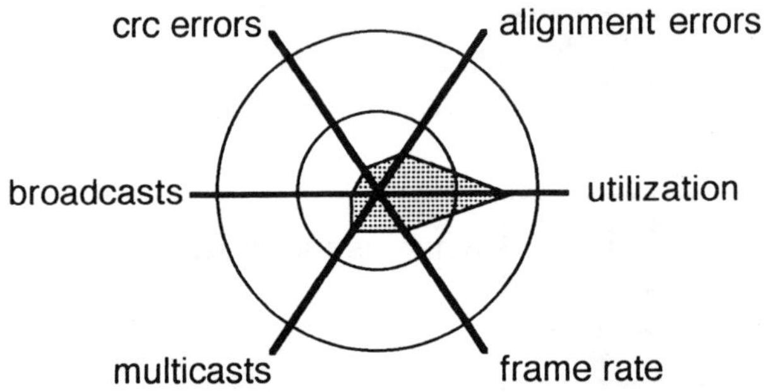

Figure 4.5
Spider diagram.

The spider diagram (spider because the axes resemble a spider's web) shown in Figure 4.5 has an axis for each of the parameters specified in the traffic policy. The inner circle represents values that are good, the middle band values that are marginal and the area outside the circles represents critical values. A polygon is then drawn on the diagram connecting the worst values for each axis found on any network segment. To show the general health of the network the polygon is coloured green if all its values are inside the inner circle, yellow if any values fall between the inner and outer circles, and red if any values fall outside the outer circle.

The spider chart clearly identifies whether or not there is a problem through the use of size and colour – as problems get worse the polygon gets larger and more eyecatching. The type of the problem is indicated by the polygon extending along the axes with unacceptable values.

Each of the spider chart axis labels acts as a button and clicking on it produces a graph that allows the value of the selected parameter to be compared across all segments.

The multisegment graph shown in Figure 4.6 has a bar for each segment and preserves the same colour scheme: values that are good are green, marginal values are yellow and critical values are red. In addition the values are sorted so that the segment with the worst value is at the top. The top segment is thus always the one whose value was shown in the spider chart.

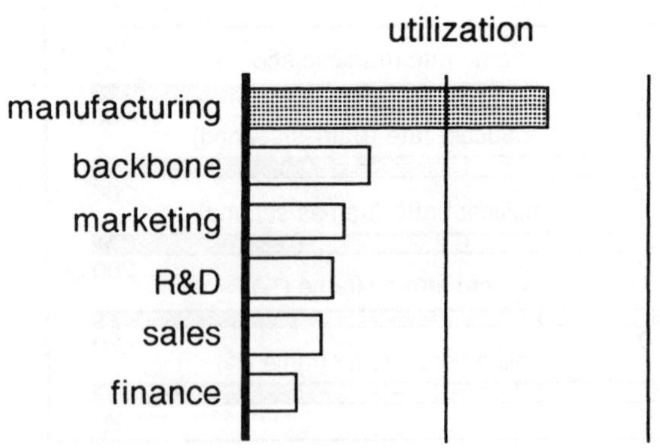

Figure 4.6
Segment utilisations.

This multisegment view clearly shows which segments are having problems through the use of colour and through position, putting the worst segments at the top.

Each segment label acts as a button and clicking on it produces a graph describing the top contributors to that bar.

The graph in Figure 4.7 shows time on the horizontal axis. Each bar represents one minute and there are 60, allowing an hour's worth of data to be seen. Each bar is broken out into its top five contributors and the rest are grouped into a category called 'other.

This top contributors' view clearly shows who is responsible for the traffic and how long they have been active. We are always given the contributors to the statistic in the multisegment view by default. There are a number of other ways of looking at the traffic on a segment and these other segment views are easily obtained.

1. Top MAC sources of frames
2. Top MAC sources of broadcast frames
3. Top MAC sources of multicast frames
4. Top MAC sources of CRC errors
5. Top MAC sources of alignment errors
6. Top MAC sources of utilisation
7. Top MAC destinations of frames
8. Top MAC destinations of utilisation
9. Top MAC pairs of frames
10. Top MAC pairs of utilisation
11. Top connections of frames
12. Top connections of utilisation
13. Segment statistics

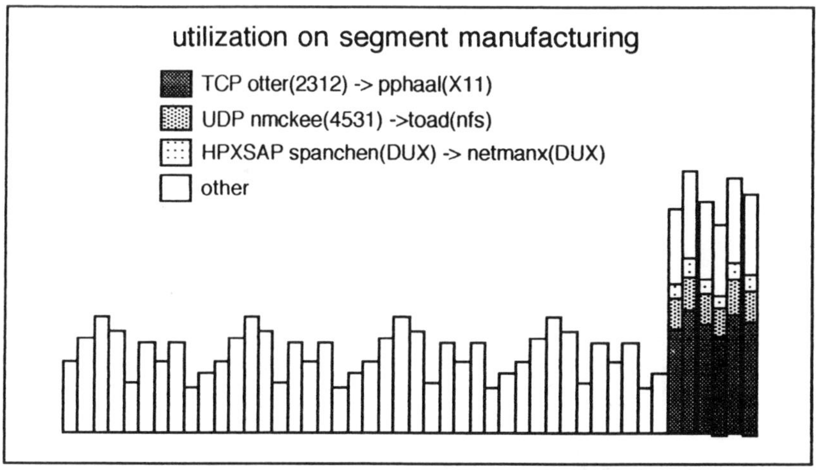

Figure 4.7
Utilisation over time.

It is sometimes necessary to compare a number of these different segment views in order to understand and identify the source of a problem.

Each contributor label acts as a button and clicking on it produces a detailed view of the contributor.

In the detailed view shown in Figure 4.8 we see the information about the different protocols, addresses, ports and applications involved in a connection between two machines. This is usually sufficient information to go to a management tool and take some action to control the problem.

4.2 Traffic control

Detecting that there is a traffic problem and identifying its source is of little value if nothing can be done to fix the problem. Using manageable network components and a good general network management map application should make a number of different control actions possible. There are a number of important features that a map application should implement for good traffic control.

Locate addresses Generally a traffic monitoring system will identify network devices by the addresses that they use when transmitting packets. Search facilities are needed so that the devices using each address can easily be located in the network map.

Administrative data Once a device has been located in the map there needs to be accurately maintained information about its physical location and where relevant the phone number of its owner or administrator. Any other information about the configuration of the device, its manufacturer, failure record etc. is also useful. It is very hard to fix a device if you don't know where it is. Many traffic problems are caused by faulty software or by mistakes by users. Being able to phone the person involved often allows the problem to be solved, and saves a lot

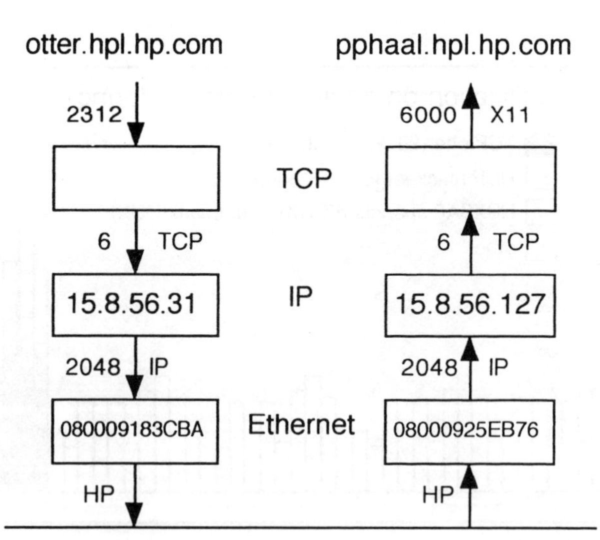

Figure 4.8
Detailed view of connection.

of walking. Some control actions disrupt network services and it is important to know who will be affected so that they can be warned.

Accurate topology Being able to see which devices are connected to one another allows the nearest managed hubs, bridges or routers to a problem to be identified. The map needs to be detailed enough to identify the specific port involved in each connection. This means that additional measurements can be made and that, if needed, control actions can be taken through commands to these devices.

Hubs A remote interface to a managed hub should allow any port on the hub to be switched off. This disconnects part of the network and is most effective if structured wiring is used so that every machine is on a separate hub port. This allows individual machines to be isolated if they are causing a severe problem.

Bridges Many managed bridges support simple filtering. Use of filters allows problem traffic to be isolated to a single segment, limiting the impact of a problem. An extreme form of action is to switch off a bridge port, isolating a whole segment from the network.

Routers Routers usually provide fairly sophisticated filtering capabilities. Again these filters can be used to limit traffic to a segment, or in extreme cases the router can be instructed to disconnect a port.

Controls that involve filtering and disconnecting parts of the network should be used with extreme caution. They can cause severe disruption to network traffic and are only an emergency measure, limiting the impact of a problem until it can be fixed. It is important to assess whether the reduced service caused by the traffic problem is better than the disruption caused by cutting off some users or services. Another thing to watch out for is that you don't accidentally disconnect the network management station from the network, preventing it from switching the device back on.

4.3 Examples

The following examples aim to give a representative sample of the types of activity involved in short term traffic management. The Resource Manager is used in these examples, and they demonstrate the way in which a task focused application can guide the user through complex problems (see Section 2.8.1). The network illustrated in Figure 4.9 is typical of many sites and will be used as the basis for the examples.

4.3.1 X-Windows

Suppose we see the display in Figure 4.10 on the Resource Manager. Our attention is caught as the diagram changes to yellow warning of a traffic problem on the network. It shows that we are having a problem with excessive utilisation on one of the segments. All the other parameters are within acceptable bounds. We use the mouse to point at the 'utilisation' label and click to get a chart comparing the utilisation on the different segments.

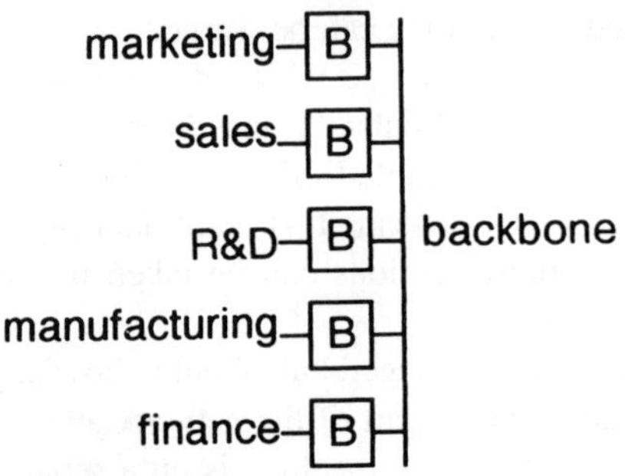

Figure 4.9
Typical site network.

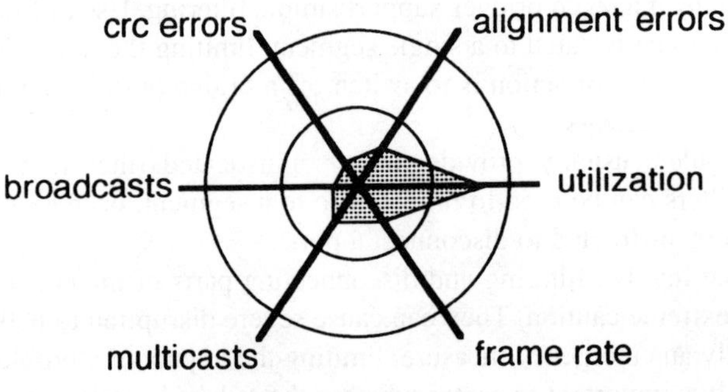

Figure 4.10
Spider chart showing excessive utilisation.

In the resulting chart shown in Figure 4.11, the 'manufacturing' segment stands out as having an unusually high utilisation. This is emphasised by its bar being coloured yellow (the other segments all have acceptable utilisations and are coloured green).

We don't yet know what is causing the problem, but we do know that it is localised to the 'manufacturing' segment. By clicking on the 'manufacturing' label we can get a breakdown of the congestion problem.

Figure 4.12 shows the utilisation on the 'manufacturing' segment over the last hour broken down by minute. We see that the utilisation has more than doubled

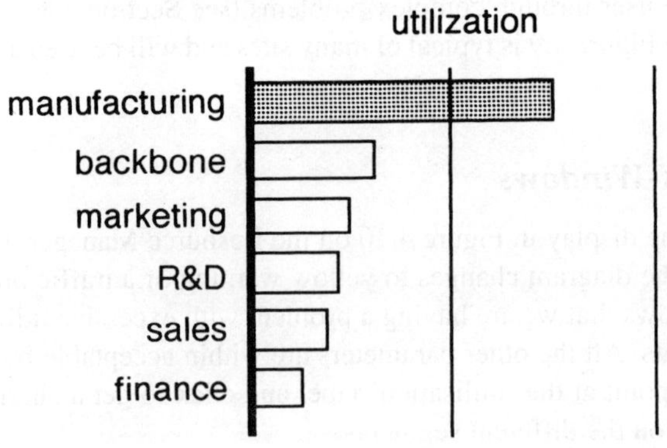

Figure 4.11
Excessive utilisation on a segment.

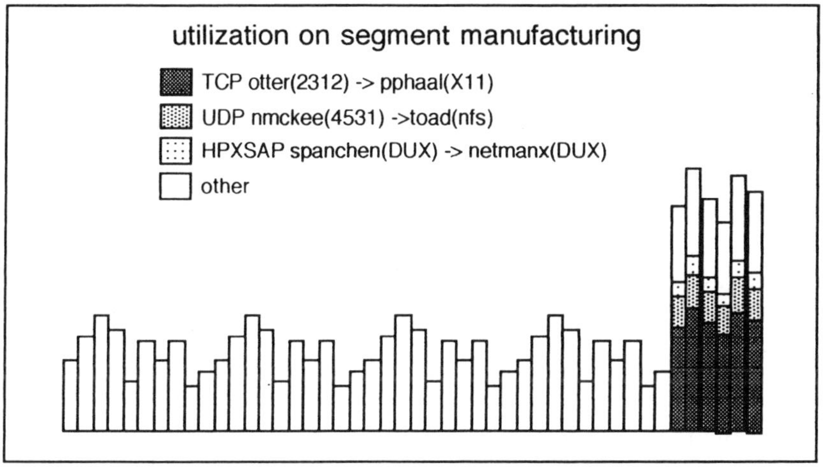

Figure 4.12
Active connections on a segment.

in the last six minutes, and that the additional traffic is due to an X-Windows session between two machines 'otter' and 'pphaal'. We can get some more detail by clicking on the 'TCP otter(2312) → pphaal(X11)' label.

This brings up the diagram in Figure 4.13 showing details of the different protocol layers involved in the connection. Because X-Windows is an application run on the client's machine it makes sense to try to call the person using 'pphaal' to find out what they are doing.

It is at this point that we need to make use of administrative information. If we look up 'pphaal' using an administrative map tool such as the Interconnect Manager we find the phone extension for this machine and call. The person using

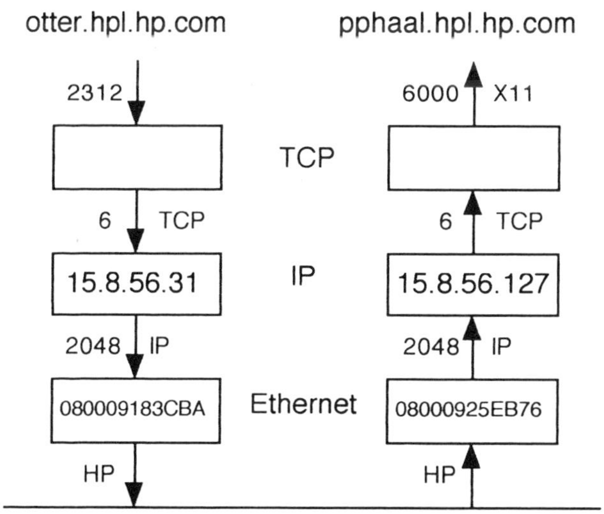

Figure 4.13
Details of active X-windows connection.

'pphaal' is embarrassed to admit that they are playing a graphical game and that this is what has been loading the network. They are happy to stop.

A quick final look at the Resource Manager (see Figure 4.14) confirms that everything is once again operating normally.

4.3.2 *Broadcast storm*

We are monitoring the network and suddenly we see that there is a problem with a high broadcast level (see Figure 4.15).

Broadcast storms can be very serious so we quickly click on the 'broadcasts' label to get a view across the different segments (shown in Figure 4.16).

Because we are operating a bridged network we see that the broadcast storm is affecting the entire site. Picking any segment, 'R&D' say, allows us to get a breakdown of the sources of broadcast activity (see Figure 4.17).

We identify 'vecab' as the source of the problem – it has suddenly started to send a continuously high level of broadcasts. In this case drastic action is required, as the broadcast storm is affecting the entire network. Broadcasts are processed by every machine attached to the network and many of the slower machines are being brought to a halt. We use the network management station to find 'vecab' and locate the hub that connects it to the network. Because this is a manageable hub we can remotely switch off the port connecting 'vecab' to the network. This immediately stops the broadcast storm.

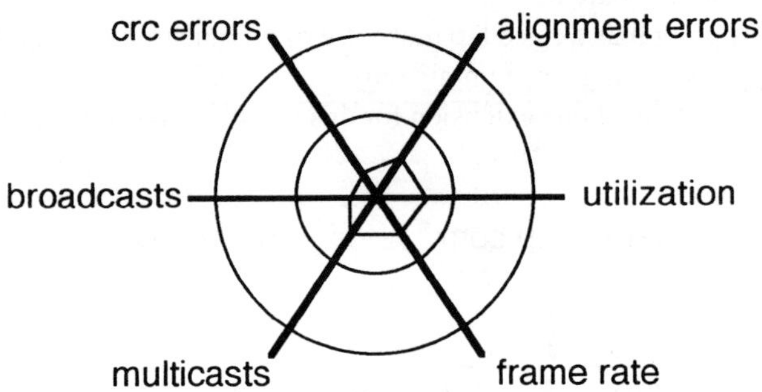

Figure 4.14
Spider chart showing everything normal.

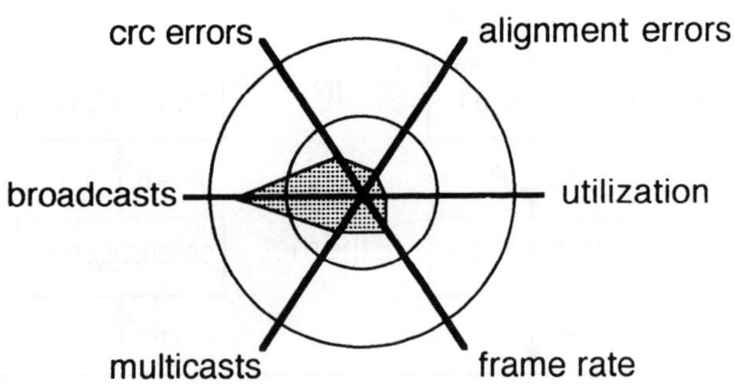

Figure 4.15
Spider chart showing excessive broadcasts.

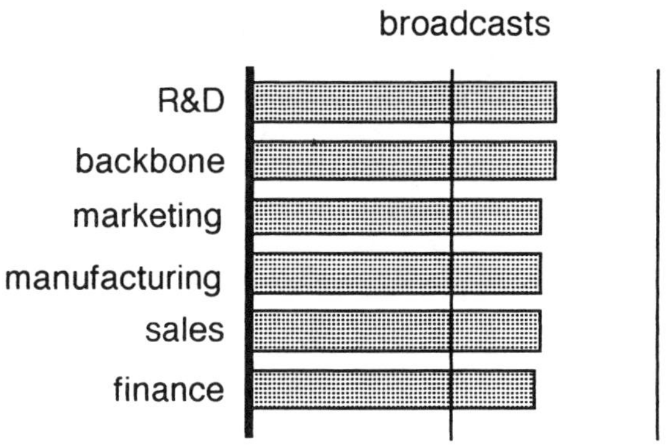

Figure 4.16
Broadcasts seen on all segments.

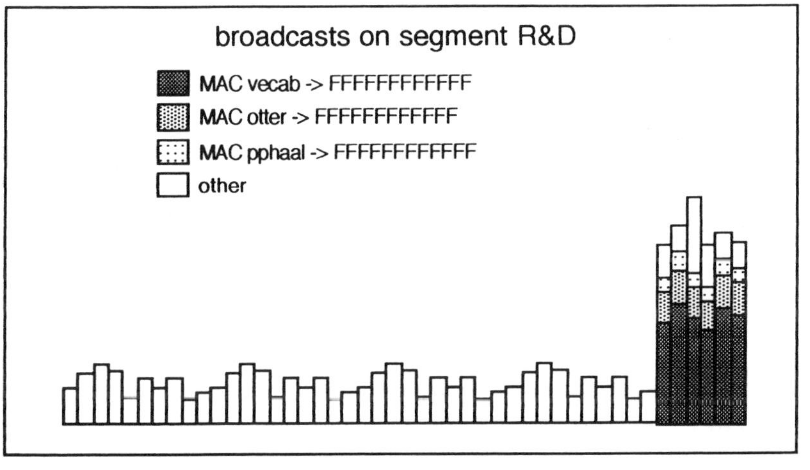

Figure 4.17
Broadcast activity on segment.

We haven't yet finished with this problem. A close examination of 'vecab' reveals a defective startup script that uses a broadcast to find a server. When no server responds it keeps trying again immediately without waiting, causing the high level of broadcasts. The script is modified so that it only tries a few times, each separated by a second, before finally giving up. Further investigation shows that other machines are using the same defective script and these machines are also fixed. At this point we can relax, having completely eliminated this problem.

4.3.3 ICMP storm

In this example the Resource Manager warns of a problem with a high level of alignment errors (see Figure 4.18).

In addition we see that the traffic levels are up in that there are moderately high frame rates on the network. The next step is to have a look at where these errors are occurring (see Figure 4.19).

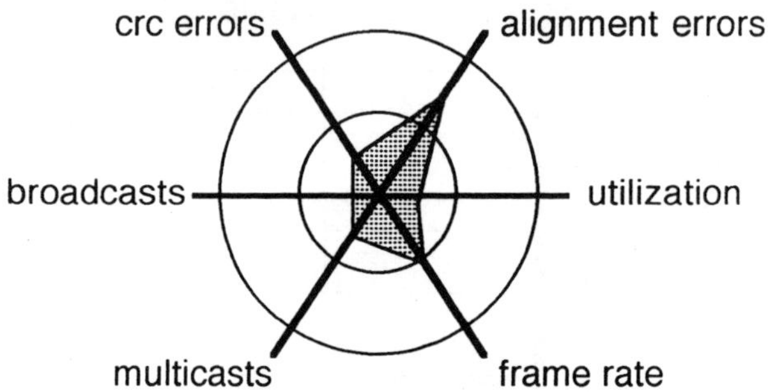

Figure 4.18
Spider chart showing high alignment error and frame rates.

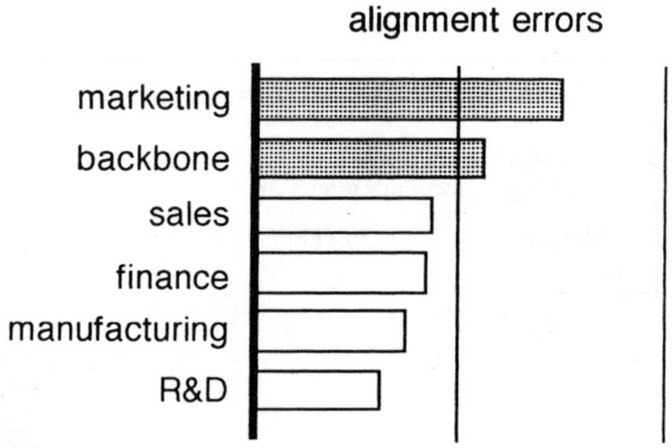

Figure 4.19
Excessive alignment errors on segments.

We can see that two segments, 'marketing' and 'backbone', are severely affected by errors. All the other segments also have fairly high error rates. This is surprising since the bridges will limit error frames to a single segment and will not pass them on. There must be some mechanism at work which is creating problems on every segment.

We click on the 'marketing' segment to look at sources of errors over the last hour.

Figure 4.20 shows us that the problem started a few minutes ago and that there are no discernible sources for the error frames. Bridges will pass traffic and we recall that there is a fairly high overall level of traffic, so let's hypothesise that the errors are caused by strange traffic activity across the network. From the error sources view we quickly pull up a view of the frame rate on the same segment.

We see, in Figure 4.21, that the frame rate suddenly increased at the same time as the high error rates, confirming that the two effects are related. Unfortunately no single connection stands out as causing all this traffic. There is one entry that does look suspicious. The ICMP (Internet Control Message Protocol) destination unreachable message is sent by a machine in response to a request for a service it does not support. In this case 'jgallow' is the recipient and must have made the request. If 'jgallow' were to broadcast such a request then everyone might

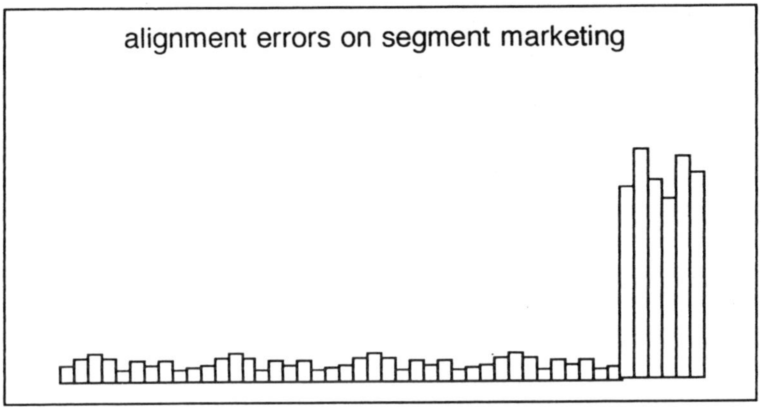

Figure 4.20
Recent increase in alignment errors.

respond, causing intense activity and errors as 500 machines try to access the network at once. To check this theory we pull up a view of the top destination of traffic (see Figure 4.22).

It looks as if we are right, all the excess traffic is destined to 'jgallow'. Correcting the configuration of this machine eliminates the problem.

This example is typical of a wide range of configuration and protocol problems that result in storms of replies. Looking at the top destinations of traffic is a general way to identify the culprit – it's almost as if every machine in the network points a finger at the guilty machine.

4.3.4 Faulty cable

In this example, shown in Figure 4.23, we see a high level of both alignment and CRC errors on the network. Unlike the previous example the traffic levels are low.

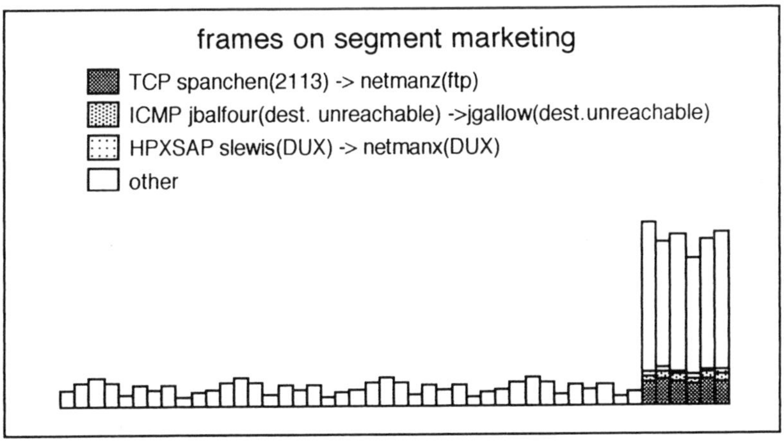

Figure 4.21
Top connections.

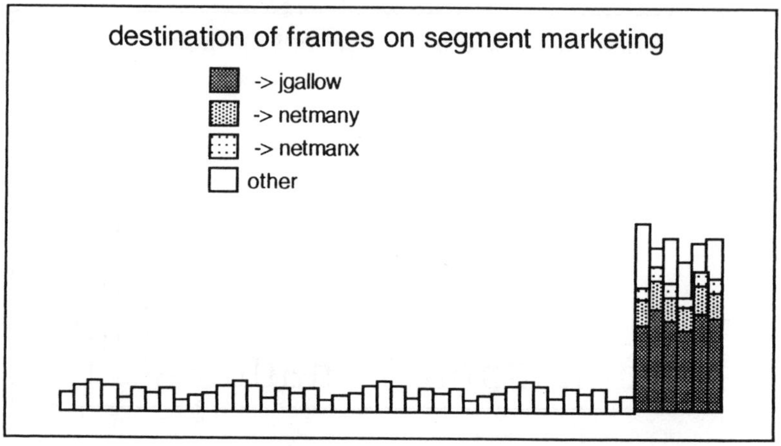

Figure 4.22
Top destinations of frames.

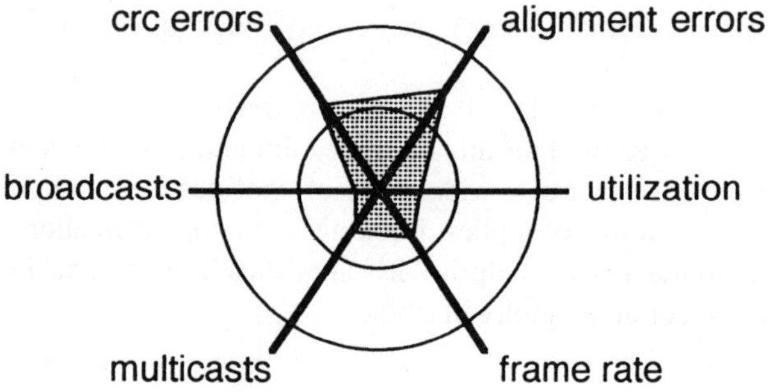

Figure 4.23
Spider chart showing high error rates.

Taking a look at where the CRC errors are occurring we pull up a view of the error rates on all the segments (see Figure 4.24).

In this case the errors are all localised to a single segment, the 'R&D' segment. The bridge is doing its job keeping these errors on the one segment. We click on the 'R&D' segment to get a breakdown of error sources.

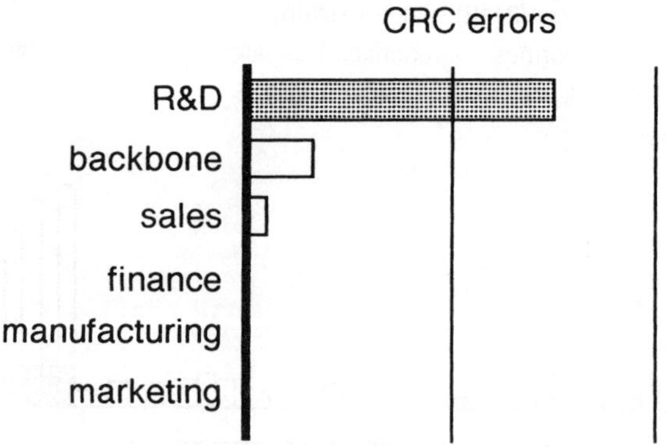

Figure 4.24
High CRC error rate on a segment.

While the graph in Figure 4.25 does not identify any single source of errors it does show that the problem occurred recently. In this case we suspect a problem with the wiring or with one of the repeaters in the 'R&D' segment.

This is a case where having manageable repeaters and a map application such as the Interconnect Manager helps save time. We can systematically check each repeater, identifying the port on which errors are being received, and we soon identify an illegal modification to the wiring in one of the laboratories in the R&D section.

If we did not have managed repeaters we would have had a long and painful search for the problem using a portable cable tester and causing lengthy disruptions to service on the 'R&D' segment.

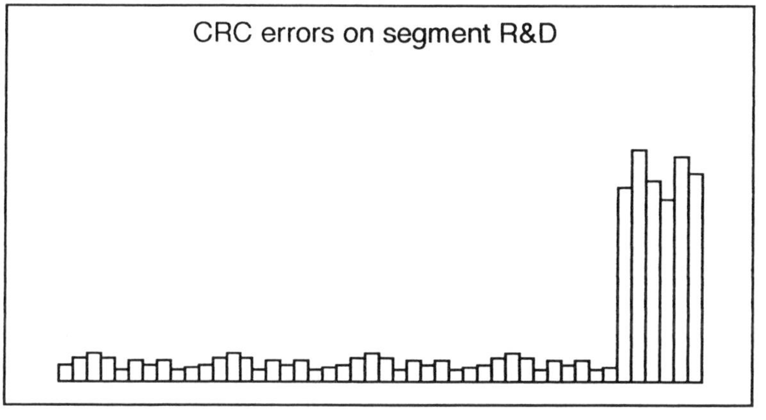

Figure 4.25
Recent increase in error rate on a segment.

5 Monitoring

Long and short term traffic management applications require detailed information about the network in order to be effective. It is the task of the monitoring activity to continuously provide this information.

Networks are large and one of the major challenges in developing an effective monitoring system is designing it so that it can scale up to realistic sizes. We need to apply the techniques introduced in Chapter 2 in order to try and reduce the complexity of the monitoring problem. Hierarchical decomposition is used to break the network up into different measurement domains. Functional decomposition determines the measurements needed for each aspect of traffic management and frequency decomposition is used to decide what monitoring intervals to use and which measurements to make at each frequency.

It is important to view monitoring as supporting applications. The monitoring system can become very difficult to build and hard to make scalable if its tasks are not well defined. Simplicity is essential. We only make those measurements that are useful to the applications and we simplify the measurement system so that it scales. The measurement subsystem can be one of the most difficult elements of the network management system to construct. Whereas the applications tend to be centralised the monitoring system tends to be distributed. It also has enormous amounts of data to sift through in order to construct the network state. If it is not constructed carefully it will be difficult to maintain and will not scale to cope with large networks.

The monitoring system is the eyes and ears of the management system. Without an effective monitoring system management is impossible. If you don't monitor you cannot manage. Also effective monitoring can greatly simplify management tasks. Often tasks that have been areas of guesswork in the past become simple if the appropriate measurements are made. When designing the monitoring system one should always be asking 'Is this the measurement I should really be making? What question does it answer? Is that question more directly answered by a different measurement?'

5.1 State and history

Key questions that need to be asked are what to measure, how often to measure and how long to keep measurements. Figure 5.1 organises the information used in the short and long term traffic management activities.

	configuration			statistics		
	component entities and attributes	intra-level relationships	inter-level relationships	single component	component pair	multiple component
application layer	mail hub	mail topology		up/down messages	mail traffic matrix	mail routes
transport layer	TCP port UDP port		service to port	up/down connections bytes	TCP traffic matrix	TCP call paths
network layer	IP address IP router IP subnet	IP topology	ports to IP address	up/down packets bytes	IP traffic matrix	
data link layer	MAC address logical segment bridge	MAC topology	IP to MAC address	up/down collisions frames	M AC traffic matrix	
physical layer	cable connector repeater	physical topology	MAC address to cable	up/down impedance noise		
geography	office building	floor plan site map	coordinates of cable runs			

Figure 5.1
State and history.

This diagram breaks down the traffic information contained in the state and history data store described in the control model (see Section 2.5).

The vertical axis corresponds loosely to some of the layers of the protocol stack. The horizontal axis breaks down the information into two main categories, configuration information and statistics. Each box contains an example of the type of information that would be associated with that layer and category. This table can be constructed for any given site based on the protocols, applications and network technologies in use on that site. The overall framework should hold for any site and provide a useful way of organising the information and identifying gaps.

The network configuration plays an important part in most network management applications. Without knowledge of the devices in the network and the way they are connected it is impossible to make any sensible decisions about changes that might be required. This configuration information is also key to interpreting any of the statistics that are collected about the network. In many ways the network configuration is the skeleton on which the statistical information hangs. While the network configuration tells you about what is out in the network and the relationships between the components, the statistics tell you about the current activities. Single component statistics tell you about the current status of each device and, looking into the past, its reliability. They also tell you how heavily loaded the device is and how likely it is to cause errors.

Component pair statistics are the traffic matrices that tell us how much demand is being placed on the network. These are the key to understanding the source of loads on the network and to taking actions to improve network performance as we saw in previous chapters.

Finally, there are measurements that we can make that characterise entire paths through the network. These are of greater interest if we are managing wide area networks where delay and line quality can be difficult to manage. For site network management these measurements are less important.

Basic network management systems do or should provide basic topology and status information. We will primarily concern ourselves with collecting statistics and with the difficult job of collecting traffic matrices for large sites.

5.2 Traffic matrices

To try to describe why traffic matrices are so important for traffic management we'll start with an example.

Imagine you are responsible for managing the road system around a city, shown in Figure 5.2. The city D has three suburbs, A, B and C, each connected by a main road.

Traffic measurements on the roads indicate that they are becoming congested and so the roads are widened (see Figure 5.3).

Widening the roads helps to alleviate the congestion, but when road users are asked whether they are happy with the results, most express dissatisfaction. To

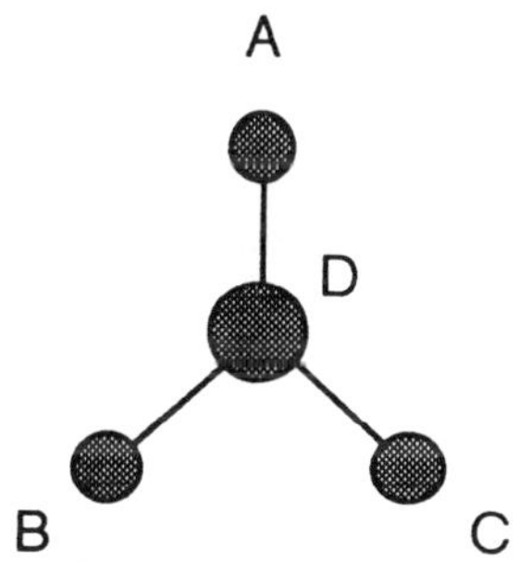

Figure 5.2
City with suburbs.

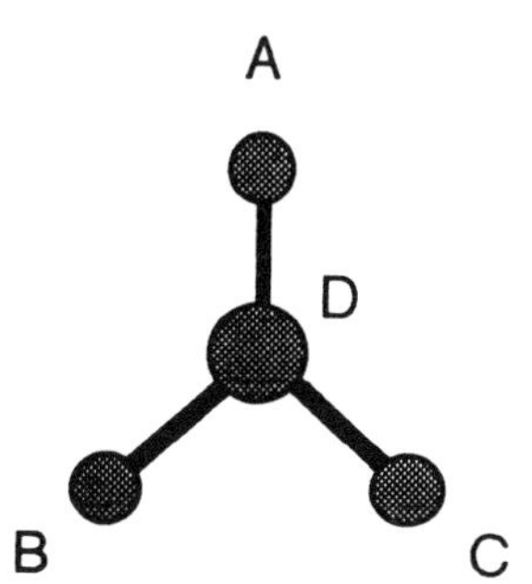

Figure 5.3
Roads widened.

find out why, a new type of measurement is performed – instead of just counting the traffic on each road a survey is performed asking motorists about their journeys. The survey asks about the start and end points of each journey. The results are combined to form a traffic matrix.

The traffic matrix shown in Figure 5.4 has a row for each starting point or source and a column for each end point or destination. The value in each square represents the amount of traffic between the source and destination. For example, the amount of traffic from A to B is 2. Another way to represent a traffic matrix is to write it as a table with one row for each square in the matrix (see Figure 5.5).

Again we can easily read off the traffic from A to B as 2. The interesting thing to notice from the traffic matrix is that most of the traffic is between the suburbs and much less goes into the city. Given this information we can understand where we went wrong. Most motorists are being forced into long journeys into and out of the city in order to travel to adjacent suburbs.

The correct solution is to build a ring road as shown in Figure 5.6. An important thing to notice is that although any measurements we make on one of the roads will change each time we change the road system (because cars will choose different routes), the traffic matrix will remain the same (because people will still need to make the same journeys). In general, designs based on traffic matrices will result in the lowest cost solutions with the best performance.

This example is analogous to the problem of monitoring network traffic. Traffic matrices provide the information needed to understand requirements so that the best network design can be selected. Traffic matrices were used in the examples involving network design in Chapter 3.

source \ destination	A	B	C	D
A	0	2	2	1
B	2	0	2	1
C	2	2	0	1
D	1	1	1	0

Figure 5.4
Traffic matrix.

source	destination	traffic
A	A	0
A	B	2
A	C	2

Figure 5.5
Traffic matrix represented as a table.

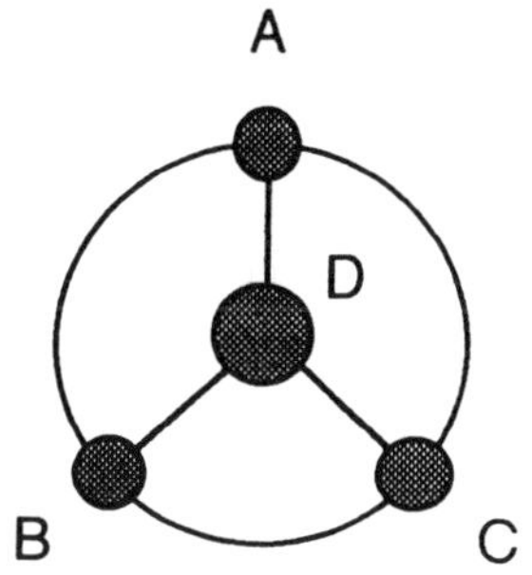

Figure 5.6
Ring road.

5.3 Top *n* measurements

While the traffic matrix is very important for long term traffic management, it is an expensive and unnecessary measurement for short term congestion management. As we saw when looking at short term management, it is sufficient to provide segment information that breaks down important segment statistics into their top contributors.

For example, if we see that a segment has a high utilisation and can find out that the top connection on the segment is a pair of machines playing a networked game, then we have all the traffic information we need in order to call up the culprits and put an end to the game.

Generally for short term management it is sufficient to know only the top few contributors to each statistic, rather than the full list of the many hundred who may each have contributed a small amount. Experience has shown that collecting only the top five in each category is usually sufficient for most tasks.

5.4 What are the important traffic measurements?

We have been looking in general terms at the types of measurement that we need for traffic management. Let's get into more detail and look at the specific measurements that we needed in order to support the long and short term LAN traffic management activities described in previous chapters.

5.4.1 Short term measurements

For short term traffic management we are primarily interested in measurements that tell us about the current level of traffic and errors in the network on a segment by segment and device by device basis. The measurements need to be made often enough, say every minute, so that we can respond quickly to traffic problems, ensuring that there is no major loss of service. These types of measurement do not need to be retained for very long, just long enough, an hour say, so that the emergence of the problem can be traced.

A useful set of measurements for short term management would include the following measurements collected from every segment, each minute and retained for the last hour.

1. Basic segment statistics, including the general statistics such as CRC error rate, alignment error rate, frame rate, byte rate, broadcast rate and multicast rate. In addition it is worth collecting statistics that relate specifically to each segment media access protocol such as collision rate for Ethernet, or average token rotation time for FDDI.
2. Top *n* measurements that allow each segment statistic to be broken down into its major components. For the general set of statistics described above we would want the following categories:
   - Top five MAC sources of frames, bytes, broadcasts, multicasts, CRC errors and alignment errors.
   - Top five MAC destinations of frames and bytes.
   - Top five MAC communicating pairs of frames and bytes.
   - Top five connections of frames and bytes.

5.4.2 Long term measurements

With long term management the primary interest is in information that tells about overall traffic patterns and chronic problems. Traffic patterns vary by time of day, but a measurement interval of an hour is usually sufficient to capture these effects. Long term management activities typically take place on a daily, weekly or possibly monthly basis, and the measurements need to be retained long enough to cover these periods. Keeping the data much longer than a month is usually not worthwhile since network traffic is constantly changing and the newer measurements are more relevant for planning.

A useful set of measurements for long term management can be logged every hour and retained for the last 31 days. They would include the same basic segment statistics that we collected for short term management, along with information on the sources of errors. The other top *n* categories, such as top five MAC sources of frames, are not required as they would be of little use over longer periods. This is because any change to the network configuration changes the traffic seen on each segment and would render these measurements meaningless. What we do want to collect are traffic matrices for all the major protocols in use on the site we are monitoring (see Figure 5.7).

Collecting all these different traffic matrices helps identify a separate class of traffic for each application on the network. This additional information makes understanding traffic flows a lot easier, as well as allowing different requirements to be met for each class of traffic.

Some of the most common protocols worth collecting as traffic matrices are listed below. A number of these traffic matrices contain additional information in the form of type or port numbers that allows the traffic to be further subdivided.

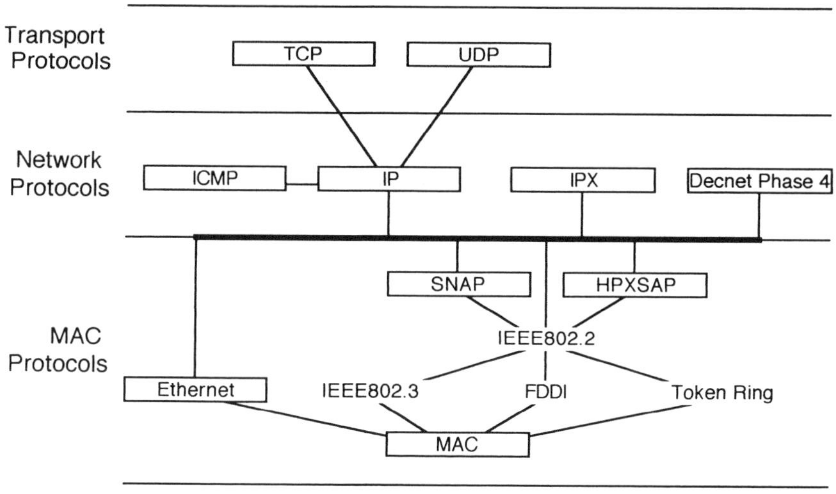

Figure 5.7
Relationship between traffic matrices.

MAC A generic MAC traffic matrix contains information about all traffic seen on all parts of the network, including Ethernet, 802.3, token ring and FDDI. The canonical form for MAC addresses is used so that traffic from all these different media types can be combined. The matrix has entries of the form:

```
source MAC, destination MAC, frames, bytes
```

Ethernet Dix (DEC, Intel, Xerox) Ethernet frame formats are more commonly used than 802.3 and contain a type field that specifies the higher layer protocol. The matrix has entries of the form:

```
source MAC, destination MAC, type, frames, bytes
```

SNAP SNAP (Sub-Network Access Protocol) is a layer on top of 802.2 which in turn can run over 802.3, token ring or FDDI. It provides the same type field as is used with Dix Ethernet and protocols running on top of SNAP will use the same type values as for Ethernet. The matrix has entries of the form:

```
source MAC, destination MAC, type, frames, bytes
```

HPXSAP Hewlett-Packard eXtentded Service Access Point is a layer on top of 802.2 and serves a similar function to SNAP. It was defined before SNAP and so doesn't use the same type values. The matrix has entries of the form:

```
source MAC, ssap, destination MAC, dsap, frames, bytes
```

IPX IPX (Internet Packet eXchange protocol) is a network layer protocol used mainly by Novell for its Netware[7] network operating system. The matrix has entries of the form:

```
IPX source, source port, IPX destination, destination port, packets, bytes
```

DECnet[8] Phase 4 DECnet Phase 4 is a proprietary network layer protocol developed by DEC (Digital Equipment Corporation). The matrix has entries of the form:

```
DECnet source, DECnet destination, packets, bytes
```

IP IP (Internet Protocol) is a network layer protocol used in many multivendor networks. The matrix has entries of the form:

```
IP source, IP destination, packets, bytes
```

ICMP ICMP (Internet Control Message Protocol) is used to provide control and management functionality for IP networks. For example, the ICMP echo and echo reply messages are used by the UNIX[9] 'ping' command to perform the loopback tests. The matrix has entries of the form:

```
IP source, IP destination, type, packets, bytes
```

UDP UDP (User Datagram Protocol) is a protocol that runs on top of IP and provides a connectionless datagram service. The application using UDP can be identified by the UDP port it uses. Popular applications making use of UDP include: NFS (Network File System), DNS (Domain Name Service) and BOOTP (BOOT Protocol). The Traffic matrix has entries of the form:

```
IP source, source port, IP destination, destination port, packets, bytes
```

TCP TCP (Transmission Control Protocol) is a protocol that runs on top of IP and provides a reliable connection service. The application using TCP can be identified by the TCP port it uses. Popular applications making use of TCP include: rlogin (remote login), FTP (File Transfer Protocol) and SMTP (Simple Mail Transfer Protocol). The traffic matrix has entries of the form:

```
IP source, source port, IP destination, destination port, packets, bytes
```

[7] Network is a trademark of Novell, Inc.
[8] DECnet is a trademark of Digital Equipment Corp.
[9] UNIX is a trademark of AT&T.

5.5 Two types of monitoring

There are two main styles of monitoring system (see Figure 5.8). In the first strategy we add monitoring capabilities in key locations in the network. If we have a problem we can then configure the appropriate devices to make a measurement which will help to diagnose the problem. We are unlikely to have monitors on every segment because they are expensive, so if a problem occurs in an unmonitored part of the network we may have to move one of the monitors. Most currently available segment monitors fall into this category. These are fairly expensive instruments that can be attached to segments in the network and make a variety of measurements. The RMON (Remote MONitor) MIB (Management Information Base) describes a standard set of capabilities and a remote interface to this class of device. The RMON MIB is described later in this chapter.

The second style of monitoring focuses on inexpensive measurements that can be made simply and cheaply. The low cost allows most segments to be monitored. These measurements are often embedded into managed network devices such as hubs, bridges and routers. The high coverage and simplicity of these measurements make it possible to construct continuous monitoring applications that will detect many types of network problem before they get serious.

It is this second style of monitoring that forms the basis of the traffic management activities. The first style of monitoring may be applied when isolating unusual problems, but should only be required occasionally.

5.6 What is statistical sampling?

Traffic matrices are vital for traffic management, but unfortunately they can be very difficult and expensive to collect. Traditionally traffic matrices have been produced on a segment by segment basis by looking at all the traffic on each segment. These segment traffic matrices can then be collected and combined later to

monitor when needed	continuous monitoring
ad hoc measurements	predefined measurements
reactive management	proactive management
high cost per segment	low cost per segment
monitor key segments	monitor most segments

Figure 5.8
Comparison of monitoring strategies.

produce a network wide traffic matrix. Instruments capable of collecting traffic matrices in this way need to be very fast in order to decode and analyse every frame, and they need to have a large amount of memory in order to store the traffic matrices. Fast instruments with lots of memory are expensive. To get continuous network wide coverage requires one instrument per segment. This is much too expensive for most sites.

An alternative technique is statistical sampling. Statistical sampling is widely used in industrial quality control, financial auditing, epidemiology and many other areas where exhaustive analysis is impossible or too expensive to perform. Sampling involves selecting and testing a small, representative group and inferring information about all the items from this group. Applying this technique to the problem of constructing traffic matrices, we still need to count every frame on the segment, but instead of decoding and analysing every frame we only examine a small randomly selected proportion of frames, say around 0.25%. This greatly reduces the speed at which the instrument needs to operate. To reduce the memory needed in the instrument we can immediately forward the samples across the network to a central location to be decoded and analysed. Site wide traffic matrices are easily produced in this central location by examining the samples from all over the network.

As networking speeds increase to 100 Mbit/s and beyond, sampling becomes the only realistic way to produce traffic matrices.

The key benefits of sampling network traffic to produce traffic matrices are:

1. **Economy** Reduced processor and memory requirements cut the cost of monitoring every segment.
2. **Timeliness** Real-time processing of samples from all over the network provides prompt alerts and responsive control.
3. **Accuracy** Sampling provides robust, accurate measurements during heavy traffic. In order to reduce costs most conventional instruments are not designed to keep up with busy networks and so produce inaccurate measurements just when they are most needed. Sampling instruments on the other hand are so simple that they can deal with high traffic rates at very low cost.
4. **Security** Instruments that look at every frame can eavesdrop on confidential information being sent on the network. This is a security problem since anyone can potentially get access to the instrument and so discover passwords and read confidential documents. Sampling on the other hand ensures that the instrument can only look at traffic patterns and cannot be misused.

5.7 Basic sampling theory

One common type of sampling is that based on time. Unfortunately this is likely to produce biased results. Imagine that there are two sources of traffic, both producing the same number of frames, but one sends them evenly over time and the other sends them in short intense bursts. A time based scheme will tend to miss the bursts and underestimate the amount of traffic from the bursty source.

If on the other hand we sample based on frame count rather than on time we can avoid this problem.

Suppose we set the sampling rate to 0.25% of frames. A simple scheme would be to look at every 400th frame on the network. Unfortunately such a regular scheme is not guaranteed to give a representative sample. If the network contained any patterns that repeated every 400 frames then clearly bias is introduced. This also applies if we sample at intervals involving common factors of 400. Clearly this is not good enough. By introducing an element of randomness to the sampling process we can avoid synchronising with any periodic patterns and so avoid bias.

An example should help to illustrate the theory behind this type of sampling. Suppose 1 000 000 frames are transmitted on a segment. A random sample of 0.25% is taken (2500 frames). If 1000 of the samples are from machine M then how many packets did machine M actually transmit? At least 1000 must have been sent because we've seen them. The most that machine M could have sent is 998 500 because we've seen 1500 that it didn't send. Neither of these two values is at all likely though. What is most likely is that 40% (1000 divided by the 2500) of the total frames are from machine M. This gives a value of 400 000 as the best estimate.

Of course it is very unlikely that machine M produced exactly 400 000 frames. Instead we can specify a small range of values that are very likely, say 95% likely, to contain the actual value. In this case we can be 95% confident that the actual number of frames sent by machine M was between 375 000 and 425 000. Another way of expressing this range is as a percentage of the most likely value, so we might say that M sent 400 000 frames +/–6%, or in other words that the largest likely error is around 6%.

Generally if we have a total number of frames, f, and take a total number of samples or observations, O, of which a certain number belong to a particular class, O_c, then we can estimate the number of frames in the class using the equation:

$$\text{estimated value} = f \, \frac{O_c}{O}$$

and the percentage error that will give us a 95% chance of including the actual value is given by the equation:

$$\text{percentage error} \leq 196 \sqrt{\frac{1}{O_c}}$$

The graph in Figure 5.9 shows the upper bound on percentage error as a function of O_c.

We can read off the percentage error for the example where O_c was 1000. This gives around 6%.

An interesting thing to notice is that the accuracy of measurements doesn't depend on the number of frames on the segment, but simply on the number of samples used to make the measurement. This property is very useful when mon-

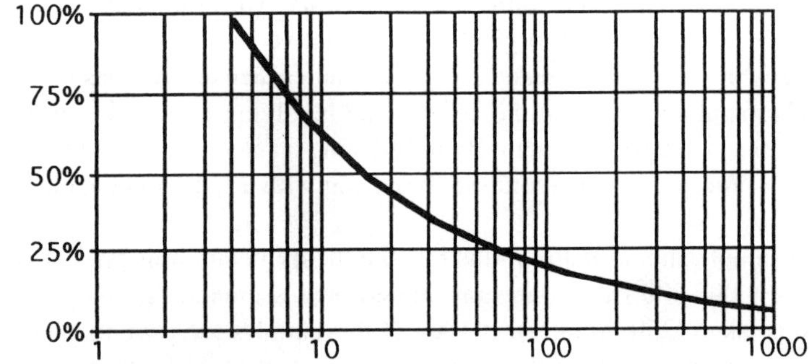

Figure 5.9
Relative error as a function of the number of samples taken.

itoring new fast network technologies. For example, suppose we are monitoring an Ethernet segment with an average frame rate of 400 frames/second using a sampling rate of 0.25%. We can get the same level of accuracy monitoring a heavily loaded FDDI ring with a frame rate of 40 000 frames/second using a sample rate of only 0.0025%. A good rule of thumb when setting the sample rate is to aim to obtain an average of around one sample per second for each segment monitored.

Statistical sampling can produce results that vary significantly around the true value when measurement intervals are short or when the traffic rates are very low. This effect is best illustrated with an example.

Suppose a machine, M, is producing one packet per second and we monitor it for an hour. M will end up sending 3600 packets in the hour. If we've set the sampling rate to be 1/400 then we should see around 9 samples from machine M. The percentage error in this case works out to be 65%. This means that we can expect to see hourly estimates of the number of packets from M ranging between around 1200 and 6000 packets.

There are two ways in which the accuracy can be improved. The first way is to increase the sampling rate. Suppose we increase it to 1/100, we should then see around 36 samples in an hour and get a percentage error of about 33% and so we would expect to see hourly estimates in the narrower range of between around 2400 and 4800 packets. Care needs to be taken when increasing the sampling rate as this also increases the amount of sample traffic on the network.

The other way to see improved accuracy is to look at the data over a longer period of time. If we were running a monthly analysis using our original 1/400 sampling rate we would expect to see around 6700 samples from M in the month. This gives us a percentage error of only 2.4% so we would be likely to see monthly estimates in the range 2 610 000 to 2 740 000 packets. Thus, we may want to use longer periods, such as weekly or monthly, to do things like billing for network usage, which may require more accurate data.

In most cases the default sampling rates should work out well. Large sources of traffic are estimated with sufficient accuracy in short intervals to make real-time congestion management effective. Longer term management makes use of longer time periods and so gives good overall accuracy.

5.8 Sampling in practice

HP EASE demonstrates a practical implementation of sampling for traffic monitoring. Sampling devices or probes are connected around the network and look at all the frames. Samples are then sent to a central sample analyser as they are generated (see Figure 5.10).

Each sample contains information about where it was collected (the probe identifier), the total frame counts at the time it was taken and the first part of the sampled frame. Only the first part, or header, is needed in order to decode the lower protocol layers and understand the traffic patterns.

The basic segment statistics such as frame count, byte count, broadcast count, multicast count, alignment error count and CRC error count are accurately maintained by the probe and passed as part of the sample 'counter values'. This means that these counts do not need to be estimated using sampling and are accurately known by the sample analyser.

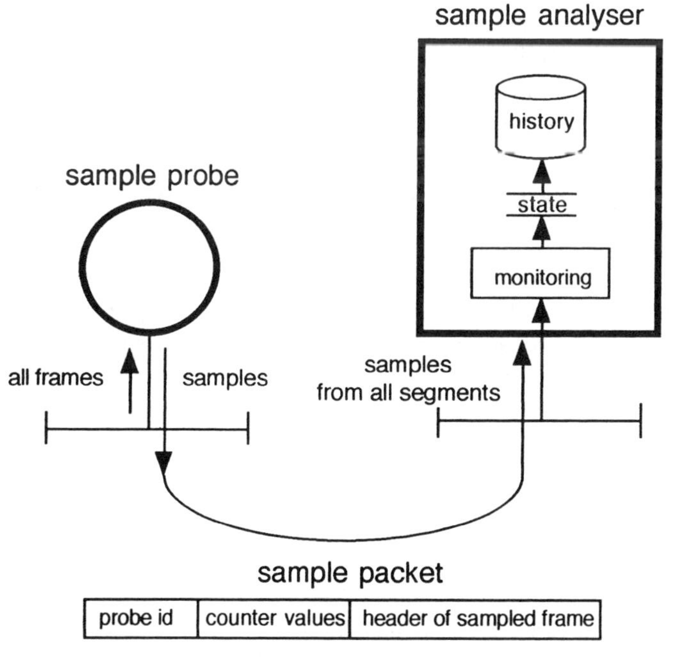

Figure 5.10
Sampling probe and sample analyser.

One area where it is obvious that sampling won't work well is in measuring unusual but serious events such as errors. Information about any errors that occur between samples is recorded and then sent with the next sample. In this way even unusual events can be accurately measured.

Control is an important consideration when building a sampling system. The sampling rates need to be controlled and the probes need to know where to send samples. The sample analyser uses a standard network management protocol, SNMP (Simple Network Management Protocol), to perform these tasks. SNMP provides a mechanism for devices with information to notify their managers. This SNMP 'trap' mechanism is used by the probes to send their samples to the sample analyser.

It is also important to make the system fail-safe. A potential problem could arise if the sample analyser were to fail or be shut down suddenly. All the probes might keep sending samples unnecessarily. By using a scheme in which the sample analyser gives the probes permission to send a certain number of samples and must keep giving further permission when they have sent their limit, it is possible to overcome this problem.

Another issue is one of fault tolerance. It makes sense to have the samplers send their samples to only one sample analyser and for the results of analysing the samples to be shared between applications. This minimises the traffic on the network and means that the computations involved in analysing the samples are performed only once. However, this creates a single point of failure. One way to overcome this problem is to have a second machine that is capable of being a sample analyser. It takes over if the primary sample analyser fails.

The sample analyser is simply a piece of software running on any general purpose computer. All it needs to be able to do is communicate with the probes using standard network protocols. The probes have slightly more specialised requirements in that they must be able to sample all the traffic on the network. Even so, they don't need to be specialised instruments, but can be part of existing network equipment such as repeaters, bridges or routers.

5.9 Location of instrumentation

Sampling is simple enough to embed in network devices and this is the most cost effective way of monitoring the network. Stand-alone probes can be used to monitor those parts of the network where the devices don't support sampling. Areas in the network connected by repeaters or hubs can be grouped together and monitored by a single probe.

Let's take the simple network shown in Figure 5.11 as an example. The circles are used to represent devices with sampling capabilities.

There are three logical segments, 'Marketing', 'Sales' and 'Backbone'. The Marketing segment can be monitored either by the one hub or by the bridge port attached to the segment. The bridge has two interfaces and is effectively two probes, one attached to each interface. The interface attached to the Backbone can be used to monitor that segment. The Sales segment needs to be monitored by a stand-alone probe because the hubs and the bridge don't support sampling.

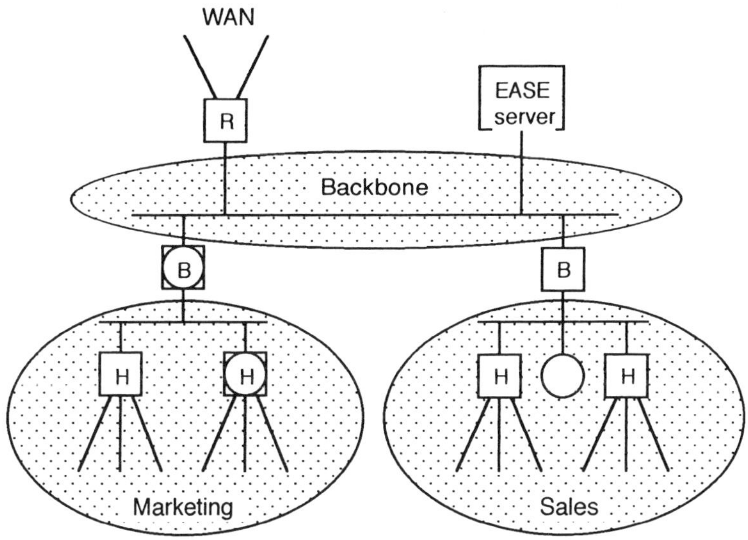

Figure 5.11
Simple network with three logical segments (H = hub, B = bridge, R = router).

The EASE server can be attached to any of the three segments and performs the sample analyser function, making the resulting traffic information available to traffic management applications. It is important that the EASE server is placed on the site so that the samples are not sent over the wide area network where they could have a significant impact on its utilisation.

EASE traffic management applications can be used on the same machine that runs the EASE server or they can be used over the network. The server performs data reductions in response to a query so that only the information needed by the application is returned. This minimises the amount of information that needs to be passed between the server and the applications, making it realistic to manage sites remotely across the wide area network.

Different people may be responsible for different aspects of traffic management. They may well be in different places.

Operational management is often performed on site because it doesn't require a great deal of expertise and the problems need to be handled immediately when they occur. In Figure 5.12 we have monitoring in two sites, 'London' and 'New York', and both sites are taking care of their own operational congestion management. Strategic management involves specialised skills. In order to reduce costs the strategic management has been centralised. The client/server architecture makes this possible.

Another benefit of this architecture is that multiple applications or versions of the same application can connect to the server at the same time. This can be helpful if there is a difficult problem and a group of people are working together to solve it.

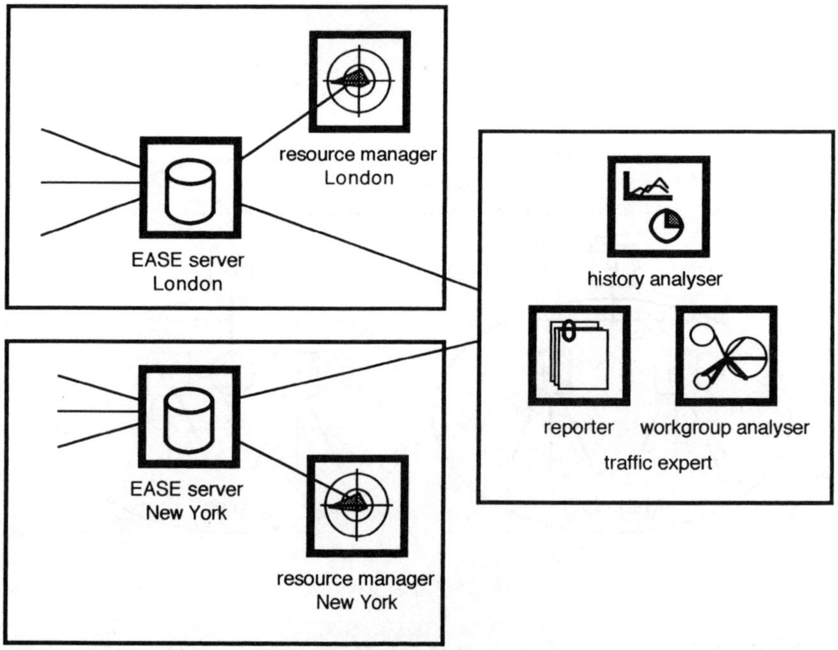

Figure 5.12
Managing multiple sites.

5.10 Monitoring with SNMP

The SNMP is the most widely accepted way of obtaining management information from devices in a multivendor network. SNMP is supported by most network equipment vendors and provides a good set of capabilities for network management. With SNMP there are two parties to an exchange, the agent and the manager (see Figure 5.13). The agent has information represented as a set of variables that the manager can access.

Access to the agent's variables is provided by a set of four basic operations:

get to get the value of a variable.

get-next used to traverse all the variables in a device.

set to set the value of a variable.

trap so that the agent can inform its managers of important events.

Providing a mechanism to access agent variables is only part of the story. The other part is to describe the variables that are available in each agent. This description is called a MIB. It has a particular structure which is best illustrated by an example:

```
SysDescr OBJECT-TYPE
     SYNTAX       DisplayString (SIZE(0..255))
     ACCESS       read-only
```

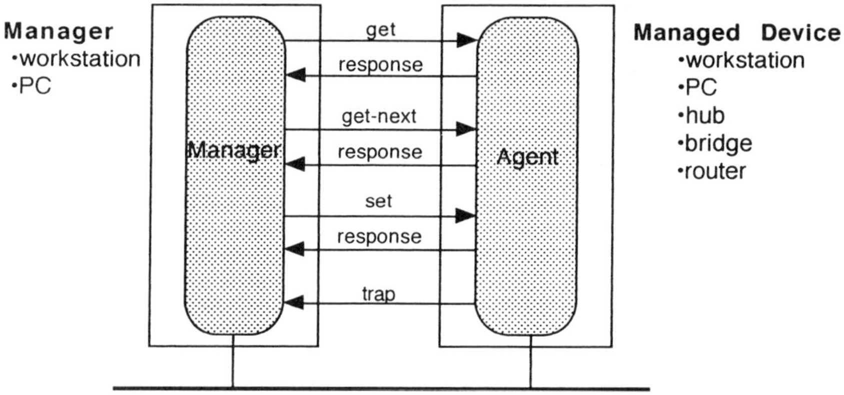

Figure 5.13
SNMP manager and agent.

```
STATUS      mandatory
DESCRIPTION
      "A textual description of the entity. This value
      should include the full name and version
      identification of the system's hardware type,
      software operating system, and networking
      software. It is mandatory that this only contain
      printable ASCII characters."
::= { system 1 }
```

This describes a variable called 'sysescr' which consists of a string of between 0 and 255 characters that describes the system running the agent. This variable is the first of the 'system' group of variables. Variables are grouped together according to function to make it easier to find their descriptions. Suppose that a bridge supports this variable and we SNMP-get its value from the bridge. We could get a result like this:

```
HP 28673A 10:10 LAN Bridge MB, EPROM code: C.01.00, RAM code: D.01.02
```

Network management applications are needed to make use of SNMP. These range from simple 'browsers' that allow variables to be read and set, through graphing packages to large platforms providing maps, continuous monitoring and alarm handling.

MIBs have been defined by a number of different standards bodies and companies. SNMP[10] has been defined by the Internet Engineering Task Force (IETF) and the protocol specification and many of the MIBs are published electronically in the form of RFCs (Request For Comment). These can often be obtained from vendors, or if you have Internet access directly from the machine 'nic.ddn.mil' using anonymous FTP. Most network management platforms will support the common MIBs.

[10] SNMP is defined by the IETF in RFC 1157.

As we have seen, it is the MIB that defines the capabilities of the device, so let's look at some of the MIBs that provide useful traffic management information.

5.10.1 MIB-2[11]

MIB-2 is a generic MIB that should be implemented by every device that supports SNMP. The main groups of interest for traffic management are:

System group The system group contains general administrative information about the device such as its description, type, uptime, administrator, name, location and function.

Interfaces group The interfaces group describes each interface on the device and contains information such as its description, type, maximum frame size, speed, physical address, administrative status, operational status, the last time it was changed, bytes received, unicast packets received, multicast and broadcast packets received, number of packets discarded on reception, number of errors on reception, number of unknown protocols received, bytes sent, unicast packets sent, multicast and broadcast packets sent, number of packets discarded on transmission, number of errors on transmission and number of packets queuing to be sent.

Address translation group Contains information about mappings between network addresses and media access addresses. This table is due to be scrapped in favour of equivalent information provided in the IP group.

IP group Contains information about the IP running on the agent machine and about whether the device is forwarding packets (i.e. is operating as a router), the time to live for packets, the number of packets received, the number of packets received with bad IP headers, the number of forwarded packets, the number of received packets that were discarded, the number of successfully processed packets, the number of packets that were requested to be sent, the number of packets that were discarded before sending, the number of times a route couldn't be found for a packet, the number of times a fragmented packet couldn't be reassembled because all the fragments weren't received in time, the number of fragments that needed to be reassembled, the number of successfully reassembled packets, the number of fragmented packets that couldn't be reassembled, the number of packets successfully fragmented, the number of packets unsuccessfully fragmented and the number of fragments created. In addition to all the counters there is information about the IP addresses that the devices uses, as well as routing table information and address translation information.

These groups can be very useful for understanding the load on individual machines. In addition the IP group gives a lot of information that helps to understand the performance of IP routers and end nodes. While MIB-2 is very general and worth knowing because of its wide support, there are specialised MIBs that contain better traffic management information.

[11] MIB-2 is defined by the IETF in RFC 1213.

5.10.2 *Ethernet,[12] Token Ring[13] and FDDI MIBs[14]*

These three MIBs add specific information about the different media access protocols to the generalised MIB-2 information. They all have statistics groups which provide useful protocol-specific statistics. Most of the statistics describe different types of network problems, and being able to understand the specific types of problem that a station is experiencing can often help to explain performance problems.

5.10.3 *Repeater MIB[15]*

The repeater MIB specifies measurements and controls for Ethernet repeaters. Repeaters are particularly useful as monitoring devices because they connect to every cable in the network. This means that they can provide information that helps to identify cable faults which could be causing performance problems. The repeater can also provide traffic information about attached machines that do not support SNMP. They can provide traffic information for their segment. Some repeaters can also supply useful topology information.

5.10.4 *Bridge MIB[16]*

The bridge MIB specifies measurements and controls for bridges. Bridges operate promiscuously and so can supply useful information about the traffic on the segments they connect to. Bridges may need to enqueue frames destined for a busy segment and if the queue becomes too full, drop them. Loss of frames through bridges produces performance problems and the bridge MIB provides information about the level of frame loss. Finally, the filtering function of bridges means that they also contain useful topology information.

5.10.5 *RMON (Remote MONitor) MIB[17]*

An RMON device must implement at least one of the following groups, or sets of functionality. The functionality is complex and the functions often require quite a bit of configuration. The basic model used is that the management station sets up a measurement, the probe performs it and then the manager picks up the results at a later time. Each measurement makes use of probe resources and since these are finite it can happen that the management station must wait for some measurements to complete before it can make new requests. Another effect of this transaction model is that many generic SNMP tools will not work with

[12] The Ethernet MIB is defined by the IETF in RFC 1284.
[13] The Token Ring MIB is defined by the IETF in RFC 1231.
[14] The FDDI MIB is defined by the IETF in RFC 1285.
[15] The repeater MIB is defined by the IETF in RFC 1368.
[16] The bridge MIB is defined by the IETF in RFC 1286.
[17] The RMON MIB is defined by the IETF in RFC 1271.

RMON devices. These general tools tend to assume that the data is always available to be read and don't support the idea of having to set up a measurement before getting the results. Special RMON tools are needed to make effective use of these devices.

Statistics group The statistics group contains statistics measured by the probe for each monitored interface. The group currently consists of the etherStatsTable (including drop events, octets, packets, broadcast packets, multicast packets, CRC or alignment errors, undersize packets, oversize packets, fragments, jabbers, collisions, and six categories of packet size distribution) but in the future will be revised to add support for other media types such as token ring and FDDI.

History group The history group periodically logs the values of the statistics so that they are available for later retrieval. It can specify periodicity and log size.

Alarm group The alarm group periodically monitors variables in the probe and compares them with thresholds that have been configured. If the monitored variable crosses the threshold, an event is generated. A hysteresis mechanism is implemented to limit the generation of alarms. It requires that the event group is implemented.

Host group The host group discovers new hosts on the network by keeping a list of source and destination addresses seen in good packets. For each of these hosts, the host group keeps a set of statistics (including packets received, packets sent, octets received, octets sent, errors sent, broadcast packets sent, and multicast packets sent).

HostTopN group The HostTopN group is used to prepare reports that describe the hosts that top a list ordered by one of their statistics. The interval over which this calculation is to be performed needs to be specified and the results are static for each report once it has been prepared.

Matrix group The matrix group stores statistics about conversations between pairs of addresses. New entries are created as new conversations are observed.

Filter group The filter group allows packets to be matched by a filter equation. These matched packets form a data stream that may be captured or used to generate events.

Packet capture group The packet capture group allows filtered packets to be captured so that they can be retrieved later.

Event group The event group controls the generation and notification of events from the device. Events can be logged or generate traps.

5.10.6 HP EASE MIB[18]

The HP EASE sampling probes are manageable through SSNMP and have a MIB that provides control of their sampling function. This MIB is used by the EASE server to configure and control the probes, and the samples are sent from the probes to the server as SNMP traps. This MIB contains no information that

[18] The HP EASE MIB is currently proprietary and defined by Hewlett-Packard.

can be used by generic SNMP tools – the traffic information is only available once the samples have been processed by the server. The use of SNMP does mean that any device supporting this MIB can be used by the EASE server to monitor traffic.

The HP EASE server provides most of the information specified by RMON and provides much more detail in the TopN and traffic matrix areas. Even if EASE is not being used most of the statistics information specified by RMON is easily obtained from managed repeaters and bridges.

The main reason for installing RMON probes would be to add management to parts of the network that have old unmanaged hubs and bridges, or because the packet capture capability is needed and the probe will be used as a remote collection point for packet analysis software.

5.11 Dispatched instruments

The routine measurements and controls needed for network management should be built into the managed hubs, bridges and routers used throughout the network. Building management functions into these devices does add to their cost and so a careful balance must be struck between the cost of implementing a function and its usefulness. Another way in which built-in management is often made cheaper is that it uses the network itself to communicate with the management applications. This provides a low cost way of managing, easy to administer, unless there is a serious problem with the network. If the network management applications are unable to communicate with the managed devices then they cease to be effective.

Portable instruments are useful for performing seldom needed or expensive measurements, or for making measurements when there are serious problems with the network that prevent any communication between the network management station and the managed devices.

Portable instruments can be attached anywhere in the network, but in order to be useful they need to be connected to the part of the network that is experiencing problems. Generally the central management system will be able to provide enough information on the type of problem and its location so that the correct instrument can be connected in the right place to be of use. For example, if we are looking for cable faults among the many thousands of cables in a large network we would start by using the network management applications to look for hubs, bridges or routers that see high error rates on any of their interfaces. We could then go and test the cables attached to these devices.

There are two main types of portable or dispatched instrument in common use, cable testers and protocol analysers.

5.11.1 Cable testers

Installation testers are used when wiring is installed to ensure that there are no problems and that the wiring meets its specifications. These instruments are generally owned by the contractors who install wiring and, as they are only used at installation, they are of limited value to a network manager.

There are other types of wire tester aimed at troubleshooting. These tend to be simple, hand-held, devices that give basic information about the activity on a cable, such as utilisation, error rates and collision rates. Coaxial cable can present special problems because there may be many points of access along its length and many machines attached to it. A single problem can affect all the machines on the cable. Common problems with coaxial cables include incorrect terminations, faulty connectors or someone disconnecting the cable. A wire tester can help find these problems by making resistance measurements or performing time domain reflectometry (TDR) measurements. A resistance measurement will indicate problems with cable breaks and incorrect terminations, and if successive measurements are made in a divide and conquer search the location of the problem can be found. The TDR measurements find the distance of the problem down the cable and so, if accurate cabling records are kept, can lead straight to the problem.

There are a few important features to look out for when selecting a cable tester for troubleshooting. Remember that this device will only be used occasionally, but when it is needed it may need to test a number of cables in different locations.

1. How portable is the instrument?
2. Is it battery powered? How long do the batteries last?
3. How long does it take for the instrument to be ready to make a measurement after being switched on?
4. How easy is it to connect the instrument to the cable?
5. How easy is it to interpret the measurements?
6. How easy is it to set up a measurement?
7. Can all the measurements, especially resistance and TDR, be made while there is still traffic on the cable?

5.11.2 *Protocol analysers*

Protocol analysers have many of the functions of a network management console, but are restricted in their view of the network to one segment. The protocol analyser can be useful if there are serious problems that make the use of the network management station impossible.

Another role for protocol analysers is to trace messages between two machines that are having trouble communicating. Decode applications display the sequence of messages and help to identify the problem. This type of function is particularly useful to developers of new network software, or when new applications are being deployed on the network and there are problems getting them to work.

A final function of protocol analysers is to generate traffic. The protocol analyser can generate loads in order to stress networking devices or to see what the effects of adding traffic to the network will be before a change is made.

Protocol analysers are increasingly being implemented as software running on general purpose computers. This has significantly reduced their cost and improved portability by allowing low cost portable computers to be used, or by allowing the software to be installed pervasively so that any machine already attached to the network can be used for protocol analysis.

Glossary

Agent An agent is a program running on a device in the network that is to be managed. It responds to commands from a manager and supplies the interface that allows the device to be remotely controlled.

Alignment error An alignment error occurs when a frame is not an integral number of bytes long.

Asynchronous transfer mode A connection oriented networking protocol particularly suited to carrying voice and video traffic. The protocol provides low latency and high guaranteed bandwidth to connections.

ATM See asynchronous transfer mode.

Bridge A device for connecting networks together. Bridges are media access layer devices and provide filtering based on MAC addresses. Bridges are often used to reduce network traffic by separating workgroups.

Broadcast Broadcasts are frames or packets that are sent to every machine connected to the network.

Cable tester A cable tester is an instrument that makes physical measurements of cables. Measurements can help find breaks in the cable or detect if it is improperly terminated.

Canonical form Depending on the media access protocol, the order of address bits seen on the network will be different. The canonical form of a MAC address specifies a particular bit order so that addresses can be compared independently of the MAC protocol.

Client The client in a client/server protocol is the machine that receives the service. For example, the client of a file server will receive files from the server.

Coaxial cable Cable with a central core surrounded by a cylindrical outer shield. Coaxial cable is commonly used in Ethernet networks and allows a number of machines to be connected without the use of a hub. Any faults in the cable will affect all the machines attached to it.

Concentrator See repeater.

CRC See cyclic redundancy code.

CRC error A CRC error occurs when the cyclic redundancy code on a received frame does not match the value that is computed from the data in the frame. This indicates that the data in the frame has become corrupted.

Cyclic redundancy code A cyclic redundancy code is a number computed from the data in a frame and is then appended to the end of the frame. It can then be used to detect any changes in the data that may occur during transmission.

DECnet A family of protocols used by computers manufactured by Digital Equipment Corporation.

DEC Phase 4 The most widely used version of the DECnet protocols.

EASE See Hewlett-Packard embedded advanced sampling environment.

Ethernet A popular local area network protocol providing inexpensive 10 Mbit/s networking. Ethernet is very similar to IEEE 802.3 and can operate on the same network.

FDDI See fibre distributed data interface.

Fibre distributed data interface A 100 Mbit/s ring based local area network protocol that makes use of fibre optic cabling.

Frame Media access protocols break data up into blocks called frames. Each frame is then separately sent on the network.

History Analyzer An HP EASE product for looking at trends in network traffic.

HP EASE See Hewlett-Packard embedded advanced sampling environment.

Hewlett-Packard embedded advanced sampling environment A family of networking products and applications that make use of statistical sampling to provide information about network traffic.

Hewlett-Packard extended service access point A protocol that runs on top of IEEE 802.3 and extends the range of higher level protocols that can be used.

HPXSAP See Hewlett-Packard extended service access point.

Hub See repeater.

ICMP See internet control message protocol.

IEEE 802.3 A local area network protocol defined by the Institute for Electrical and Electronic Engineers that provides 10 Mbit/s networking. An 802.3 network is very similar to Ethernet and can operate on the same network.

IETF See Internet Engineering Task Force.

Interconnect Manager A network management product from Hewlett-Packard that has facilities for discovering and displaying network topologies and for controlling hubs, bridges and routers.

Internet The Internet is a world-wide nework connecting many academic and industrial organisations. Widely used protocols such as IP and SNMP have been developed by the Internet.

Internet control message protocol A protocol used to control and manage IP networks.

Internet Engineering Task Force The group within the Internet that develops the protocols used on the network.

Internet packet exchange protocol A network level protocol used primarily in Novell networks.

Internet protocol A network level protocol developed and used on the Internet and widely used for large corporate and academic networks.

IP See Internet protocol.

IPX See Internet packet exchange protocol.

LAN See local area network.

Local area network A network confined to a limited geographical area. Popular local area network protocols include Ethernet and Token Ring.

MAC See media access layer.

MAC address The address used by the media access protocol that uniquely identifies a machine attached to the network. In local area networks MAC addresses are typically six bytes long and the addresses are administered by the Institute for Electrical and Electronic Engineers (IEEE).

Management information base A description of the functions that an agent can provide.

Manager A program that communicates with agents in the network in order to monitor and control the networked devices.

MAU See media access unit.

Media access layer Provides the protocol needed to transfer frames of data from one interface to another. The protocol controls access to the network and ensures that data corruption is detected. Common media access protocols are Ethernet and Token Ring.

Media access unit Connects the network interface to the cable, ensuring that the appropriate signals are generated for the cable type.

MIB See managment information base.

Multicast Multicast frames or packets are sent to a group of machines on the network all sharing the same multicast address.

Network File System A protocol used to access remote file systems. Network File System was developed by Sun Microsystems. It is widely deployed and implementations are available for most types of computer.

Network layer Provides the protocol needed to transfer packets between different neworks. Routing is an important function of the network layer. Popular network layer protocols are IP and IPX.

NFS See Network File System.

Optical fibre Glass or plastic fibres used to carry data transmitted as light.

Packet Network-layer protocols break data up into blocks called packets. Each packet is then sent separately across the network.

Physical layer Defines the physical dimensions of connectors and the signals used to send data so that machines can be connected.

Protocol The sequence of messages and responses needed to send data on a network. The protocol also specifies the format of the messages so that both machines will be able to interpret their contents.

Protocol analyser An instrument used to follow the sequences of messages making up a protocol exchange. As well as following messages protocol analysers can collect statistics about overall traffic levels on the network.

Repeater A device for regenerating the electrical signals so that cables can be connected together to form larger networks. Repeaters can help to isolate physical problems so that they do not affect the rest of the network.

Reporter An HP EASE product that periodically reports on network traffic.

Resource Manager AN HP EASE product that shows a real-time view of network traffic levels, traffic sources and error sources.

Router A device for connecting networks together. Routers are network layer devices and provide filtering and routing based on network addresses.

Server A server in a client/server protocol is a machine that provides a service. For example, a file server will make available its file system to its clients.

Simple Network Management Protocol A protocol used to communicate management information and instructions between managers and agents in the network.

SNAP See Sub-Network Access Protocol.

SNMP See Simple Network Management Protocol.

Structured wiring Network cabling organised in a hierarchical way using patch panels so that changes can easily be made.

Subnet A group of network layer addresses that form a single logical group for the purposes of routing.

Sub-Network Access Protocol A protocol used to encapsulate the differences between the different media access protocols.

Subnet mask The subnet mask is a bitmask used to separate the subnet part of an IP address.

TCP See transmission control protocol.

Token Ring A ring based protocol providing 4 or 16 Mbit/s networking. Primarily used by IBM protocols.

Traffic Expert An HP EASE product for analysing traffic patterns and for tuning network topologies.

Traffic matrix A matrix in which the amount of traffic between each pair of networked machines is recorded.

Transmission control protocol A protocol running on IP that provides a reliable byte stream between two machines.

Topology The way in which the network components are connected.

Twisted pair Pairs of wires twisted together. This type of wiring is used for telephones and extensively for networking.

UDP See User Datagram Protocol.

User Datagram Protocol A protocol running on IP that provides an unreliable message service.

WAN See wide area network.

Wide area network A network covering a large geographical area, typically tens to hundreds of miles.

Workgroup A group of networked machines that communicate extensively together. Most typically a server and its clients.

Workgroup Analyzer An HP EASE product that displays traffic patterns so that problems with network partitioning can easily be seen.

X-Windows A popular windowing sysem developed by MIT that has the capability to open windows between machines across a network.

Index